A mother's story of grief and grace
in the face of her daughter's mental illness

*"This book is a powerful tool for parents, child advocates and policymakers who are calling for greater cultural competence in the delivery of mental health services. This mother's story reveals the double jeopardy faced by many, many families of color due to ignorance and stigma associated with mental illness, and a system that is ill-prepared to provide appropriate care."*

— **Tamara Lucas Copeland**, former President, Voices for America's Children

*"**Losing Control: Loving a Black Child with Bipolar Disorder** is a mother's eloquent and passionate homage to her daughter Maya and to the journey the two of them take in search of peace and health. This is a powerful family narrative written by a brave and fiercely tenacious parent, a person of color who by herself, pushes through a mental health system essentially unfriendly and unhelpful, yet masked by friendly rhetoric. There are no happy endings here; however, this book is a treasure chest for parents of all cultural backgrounds as they seek guidance and answers concerning their children's mental illness. The information, insight, and reflections about this mother–daughter journey are a must read for parents, practitioners and policymakers."*

— **Dr. Michael A. Carrera**, Director, The Children's Aid Society
National Adolescent Sexuality Training Center

# Losing Control

Published by Advantage, Charleston, South Carolina.
Member of Advantage Media Group.

ADVANTAGE is a registered trademark and the Advantage colophon is a trademark of Advantage Media Group, Inc.

Printed in the United States of America.

ISBN: 978-1-59932-060-1
LCCN: 2007939588

Most Advantage Media Group titles are available at special quantity discounts for bulk purchases for sales promotions, premiums, fundraising, and educational use. Special versions or book excerpts can also be created to fit specific needs.

For more information, please write: Special Markets, Advantage Media Group, P.O. Box 272, Charleston, SC 29402 or call 1.866.775.1696.

# Losing Control

## Loving a Black Child with Bipolar Disorder

### Cassandra L. Joubert, ScD

with Linda Thompson Adams, DrPH, RN, FAAN and Jan Hutchinson, MD, MPH

*Advantage*™

*To Maya Mandela —*
*with all my love*

# Contents

# *Acknowledgements*

When I look back over the many years of struggle and heartache, the memories that remain a deep source of hope for me today are of the people that loved and reached out to help me. Perhaps first and foremost is my sister Pam, who was always there to listen to me, encourage me, and cry with me. She has been there for me spiritually every day that I can remember, and to her I am most grateful.

During those early years in Flint, Michigan, when life was so confusing and painful, my employer was empathetic, flexible, and supportive. Without support at such a critical time, the success story I am sharing would not be possible. I extend deep gratitude to Dr. Velma Allen, President, Mott Children's Health Center for her help and support.

Steve and Marcia, Karen and Joe, Gail, Shelley, Janet Z., Rosie, Sharnita, and Dondeena – thank you for helping me care for Maya over the years. Your love and support will never be forgotten.

To Max Taylor, PhD, Darlene Bliss, MSW, Ann Renard, PhD, and Desanka Stipic, MD, thank you for the warm and comforting face you put on a very challenging mental healthcare system. Your competent and constant care and support have been life-saving.

To the members of the interdisciplinary support team at Groves High School in Birmingham, Michigan, especially Kathy Dittrich, Brian Wolcott, and Mary Lee, thank you. You saved my daughter's life.

Thanks to Brenda Gilchrist for her expert editing support.

I extend deep gratitude to Terri D. Wright, MPH of the W.K. Kellogg Foundation, whose devotion, expertise, and encouragement made this book possible—my deepest gratitude.

To my amazing son Josh, thank you so much for never complaining, always understanding, and for loving and supporting your sister. I love you more than you could ever know. You are my best buddy!

And to my dear husband Michael Allen, thank you for being my anchor and my lifeline, and for reminding me to just breathe and connect with the presence of God. You are my reward. I will love you always, my King.

# *Foreword*

Pediatric bipolar disorder is a highly controversial diagnosis. The diagnosis has taken the same route as childhood depression, which was unaccepted as a viable diagnosis until the early 1970's. While families are devastated by the disorder and school programs are destroyed by these children in the classroom, we are anxious about acknowledging the diagnosis that is staring directly at us. We miss the diagnosis because of the variability of symptoms and because practitioners do not have a template from which to diagnose. Symptoms shift from one developmental phase to another. We treat it, at times, as "severe" ADHD or depression, and our medications of choice often exacerbate the symptoms.

We need books such as Losing Control to chronicle the developmental pathways of bipolar disorder. It is rare to find books that follow a child from infancy through his or her development. Such books enable us to view the earliest indicators of the disorder and enable parents to be alert for these early warning signs.

Dr. Joubert has taken this a step further and has enabled us to see that pediatric bipolar disorder manifests itself similarly in the African-American population to the way it does in the Caucasian population. The disease has no cultural boundaries. However, the rules of each culture determine how the disorder will be defined and treated.

In the literature to date, the cultural aspects of pediatric bipolar disorder have not been highlighted, so the disorder has been seen primarily as a disorder in Caucasian families in the same way that autism, in the 1960s, was seen as a disorder in white families of high intelligence and high socioeconomic status. The "refrigerator mothers" who were seen as the cause of autism were white. If an African-American child manifested the same symptoms as a Caucasian child, he or she would receive a different diagnosis and different treatment. The African-American mother could not even have the "status" of a "refrigerator mother."

This is the clear danger of ignoring cross-cultural commonalities. The black child who evidences the symptoms of pediatric bipolar disorder is seen as being oppositional, with perhaps a conduct disorder or worse. But these diagnoses result in misdiagnosis and mistreatment of these children. Dr. Joubert has alerted us to the fact that we need to be very careful in our assessment of the African-American child who is evidencing symptoms suggestive of a mood disorder, and courageously shares her journey with her own child with us.

In addition to opening our eyes to the disorder in her culture, Dr. Joubert presents a powerful narrative that illustrates professionals' problems in making the correct diagnosis and developing treatment plans that address the disorder. She also invites us into her family to see the difficulty in gaining support from family members who see her as an inadequate mother. Each of these problems is cross-cultural and must be brought to light.

In the year 2007, we are failing these children and their families by not providing professionals with the training to diagnose the disorder correctly, and parents and professionals often have an adversarial relationship with schools that are unprepared to deal with these children and call them something different in order to provide inadequate services. Dr. Joubert is courageous in making it clear that we must do better.

This is a profound story that we all need to read to get angry enough to band together and demand better psychiatric, psychological, and educational services for our children, particularly those who are culturally in the minority. I applaud Dr. Joubert for sharing her and Maya's story. It is a story of courage, persistence, and the refusal to surrender in both parent and child, and it will surely pave the way for families from different cultural groups to be similarly courageous in order to get the services that their children need.

Ira Glovinsky, Ph.D.
Author, *Bipolar Patterns in Young Children*

# SECTION ONE:

## *Loving, Parenting, and Praying*

by Cassandra Joubert, ScD

*I still grieve for my child. Even today, when she greets me with a hug or a kiss, I still feel the pain of all the lost years, all the agony, all the wildness, and all the fear.*

*Yet, who she is today is a rebirth, a second chance, filled with hope and anticipation, albeit only a shadow of what she could have been, what we could have been.*

*But shadows are sneaky little things. The secret is in knowing they never completely control the day. Nor do they control our tomorrow.*

*God is in charge. I release and I let go ... I'm giving up control.*

# I. A Wanted and Planned Child

My second pregnancy was planned to perfection ... well, almost. Being the master planner of all that would occur in my life, I decided I would space my kids four years apart so that I wouldn't have two in college at the same time. My mother had always told me, "You can't plan your life. You have absolutely no control over what happens to you." Yet, I was determined to prove her wrong. The last two lines of my favorite poem Invictus had etched themselves in my mind while I was in high school: "I am the master of my fate, I am the captain of my soul," and this view was more in keeping with the life I intended to create. And with Plan A already three years in full swing, it was time to execute Plan B.

Plan A resulted in a happy and energetic little boy who nursed at my breast until he was almost two. But according to my mother, he wasn't supposed to be born. Ever since I was a young preteen who gathered up all the preschool kids in the neighborhood and read them stories, my mother had said, "You'll never have kids of your own because you want them too much." Despite her ill-fated predictions, I had given birth to a very healthy baby boy, and I would prove her wrong again by not only planning this pregnancy to the letter, but by birthing the daughter of my dreams.

Having failed the "guess the gender" test with my son, whom I had been absolutely sure was a girl from the moment he was conceived, anxiety set in. I had confidently called him "Maya" while he was in utero. As I lay on the delivery table and heard the doctor say, "It's a boy!", I had let out a sad sigh of disbelief. "A boy?" I retorted. How on earth could this be? My husband already had two boys from his first marriage, I thought to myself, and I had promised him a girl! And having always been so successful at planning my life, my humble prayer for a little princess was sure to be granted. Determined that our marriage would be different from his first marriage in every way, including giving birth to the girl he'd always wanted, I believed God was on my side.

So, there was just no way fate would trick me, the master planner. My princess would be born in spring, I calculated, just when the tulips and azaleas were blooming. And perhaps the dogwoods would be springing forth too or the giant zinnias we always planted in the front flowerbed of our Oklahoma home. I wouldn't gain as much water weight as had occurred with my son who had been born in the harsh heat of a Tulsa summer. No, this pregnancy would be perfect in every way—a pretty little girl who would nurse at least as long as her brother, filling me with the same incredible feelings of love and purpose that his suckling had brought.

When I missed my period that summer before she was born, it was a sure bet I was pregnant. Regular periods had been the norm all of my life, and the only other time I had missed a period was with my first pregnancy. My periods were awful—extremely painful and disruptive. So pregnancy was a great source of relief! I couldn't wait until the first prenatal visit, which all of my graduate school training had told me should happen as soon as possible after conception. I called the doctor's office to schedule the first visit, already yearning for the thrill of caring for a tiny, new baby.

My husband John was very attentive in those early days, eager to help and do things I desired, so, of course, he agreed to accompany me to the first prenatal visit. I'll never forget the charmingly bright blue shirt he wore that day. It was so strikingly lovely against his dark chocolate skin. Perhaps the baby's room should be accented with this color, I thought.

Our previous obstetrician had decided not to continue her practice, so one of her former partners would deliver our baby this time. When the doctor walked into the exam room on that first visit, he politely said hello and gave me a limp handshake. Then he turned to look at my husband seated at the end of the exam table. Being so proud that John had come along on the visit, I expected the doctor to welcome my husband warmly and express some degree of satisfaction that a father would be so involved this early in a pregnancy. Instead, he threw his head back in surprise and smirked, "Wow, that shirt is bright enough to blind me." What amazing bedside manner.

Although I felt myself becoming angry that he would say such a thing, in my usual way with white folk those days, I didn't let my anger show. When I was ten years old, five white boys speeding through our segregated black neighborhood threw a stream of Clorox out of their car window and right into my eyes as I walked down the street with my friends. Screaming in pain and temporarily blinded by the attack, I had vowed that day to never forget what it was like to grow up in the hate-filled south. But now, I just couldn't let this doctor's pea-brain comment overshadow the excitement I felt about my first prenatal exam. I was too eager to learn how this little baby was growing inside of me.

By the second prenatal visit, I was feeling sick from morning to night, day in, day out. Nothing stayed on my stomach except Cream of Wheat, and I had lost seven pounds. Having decided not to see that doctor again, I chose a female partner in the practice. With a woman, albeit a white woman, I was confident I would receive compassionate and sensitive care.

When she walked in the exam room on the second prenatal visit and asked how I was feeling, I described my non-stop nausea. By now I was past the first trimester when nausea usually subsides, but still, I was unable to keep anything on my stomach. She thought for a moment, and then asked if my pregnancy had been planned. I assured her it had been planned to the minute. She then carefully explained that some women have an unconscious resentment about being pregnant which leads them to subconsciously reject the pregnancy. This subconscious rejection, she explained, could come to the surface as physical symptoms.

After a moment, what she was implying really sank in. I was floored! Being a mother was all I had ever really wanted. I had voluntarily stopped taking the pill four months prior in order to get pregnant. There was no doubt that this baby was wanted and planned. I was a longstanding member of the Board of Directors of our local Planned Parenthood and had been an advocate for "wanted and planned" pregnancy since my college days. Why on earth would she suggest that I hadn't wanted to be pregnant?

At that moment, I remembered a conversation with a nurse at that same medical practice years ago when I was pregnant with my son. The nurse asked what pregnancy this was for me, and I told her it was my first. She paused and repeated the question, "I mean, how many times have you been pregnant before this pregnancy?" And I'm thinking, why would this nurse believe that a person with a doctorate from Johns Hopkins University might not understand her question? Had she asked what was my gravida and parity (which was medical terminology for the number of previous pregnancies and births); I could have answered that as well. Again, I replied, "None." Although she seemed not to believe me, she wrote "Gr0, Para0" on the medical chart.

Are women treated with this kind of disrespect in physicians' offices all the time, I wondered? Was it because I was a twenty-seven-year-old black woman who had never been pregnant before? Was I contradicting stereotypes of black women's promiscuity, or the belief that we use abortion as contraception? I asked myself, isn't it funny how the many years of subtle and not so subtle racism had caused me to "go there"?

Now, three years later, I was being treated poorly again. My integrity was being questioned, and my honesty was in doubt. Or was I simply being paranoid? It didn't matter. Regardless of what this doctor chose to believe, my pregnancy was indeed both wanted and planned.

Over the next several months, I felt just horrible. The nausea was a constant companion. The doctor prescribed Vistaril, but knowing the possible danger of taking drugs while pregnant, I only took the little capsules when I absolutely couldn't bear that sick-to-my-stomach feeling. I continued to go to work each day, sometimes darting out of business meetings to throw up, or to find my way to the lower level office lounge to nap for a few minutes. My boss Phil was extremely empathetic, commending me for coming to work and performing well despite not feeling up to it. I rationalized that going to work was easier than being nauseous at home. At least I had great projects to distract me when I was at work. Despite still being sick seven months into the pregnancy, the doctor had said I wouldn't be nauseous once the baby was born. To me, this just didn't seem possible. After living through nine months of constant nausea, it seemed I would never feel normal again.

I worked right up until the weekend before Maya's birthday. And remarkably, by the time she was born, I had managed to gain the recommended twenty-five pounds.

Labor began just after midnight on March 23, 1987. The day before, I had waddled around our cul-de-sac, joking with my neighbors that I was going to will this baby's birth that very night. Consistent with my ability to plan my life, I went into labor around midnight.

Less than thirty minutes after my labor began, my water broke and I called the doctor. I woke my husband who had been sleeping spoon-like beside me. Things were happening unbelievably fast. With my son, labor began slowly with mild contractions, and they were pretty weak for almost thirty-six hours. Back then, the doctor had sent me home because when I arrived at the hospital I had only dilated two centimeters, despite twelve long hours of contractions ten minutes apart.

When we arrived at the hospital with this second baby, I was already in "transition," an advanced stage of labor. When the nurse tried to get the hospital gown over my head, I said softly to her, "Please don't touch me."

She yelled out, "Get the resident! The doctor's not gonna make it in time!" They wheeled me into the delivery room, got me up on the delivery table, and when I asked for the anesthetic, the nurse said, "It's too late, honey. By the time the meds take effect, the baby will already be here."

Damn! While I had expected a completely natural childbirth the first time, I developed pre-eclampsia and required Pitocin to induce my labor. Then they had to give me an epidural to manage the hard, drug-induced contractions. This time around, I had given up on the possibility of a natural birth and fully expected to have those wonderfully relaxing drugs. Now I was being told that things were moving too quickly. This, I thought, was definitely not according to plan.

At about 2:20 a.m., my beautiful baby girl was born. She weighed 7 pounds, 3 ounces, and had Apgar scores of 9 and 9. She also had a full head of straight black hair, and looked like a little papoose. All the lay "experts" said her full head of hair explained the nine months of nausea. Whether this was folklore or science, it didn't matter now. At last, my dream of having a girl had come true, and my master life plan was being superbly executed. I placed her immediately on my breast. Unlike her brother who sucked ferociously the minute he was born, she barely suckled the breast and hardly opened her eyes. Not five minutes after she was born, a nurse offered my husband, who had been by my side during the very brief but brutal delivery, the opportunity to bathe her. He eagerly agreed and the three of them took off quickly down the hall.

She had only been with me for two minutes when they had whisked her away! "Whose baby is this anyway?" I asked myself impatiently. I laid there alone in the delivery room for what seemed like an hour, becoming more frustrated with each passing moment. When her father finally returned with her, he was singing, "*Here comes Peter Cottontail, hopping down the bunny trail ...*" I could hardly wait to get her to my breast again. She very gently suckled for a minute or so, and then, almost instantly, fell soundly asleep. At that moment, after what had seemed like a lifetime of misery, I no longer felt sick, no nausea, no pain, just the anticipation of new joy.

# II. A Sleepy and Easily Annoyed Baby

Lots of babies don't sleep through the night and suffer with colic, and I was well prepared for this possibility. My son had been a colicky baby, and did not sleep through the night until he was eighteen months old. I was so fatigued and stressed during his infancy that my hair fell out in small, neat patches. But never for a moment did I not absolutely adore my time with him as an infant and a toddler.

In fact, it had been my overwhelming joy in raising him that had led me to want another child, and I was totally enamored with the thought of breastfeeding again. I had dreamed of breastfeeding even as a young girl playing with dolls. At my first gynecological visit at the age of fourteen, I asked my doctor whether I would be able to breastfeed. His look of surprise told me that such a question was unusual for a girl my age. "Do you want to breast feed?" he asked. I nodded enthusiastically that it looked fun!

When Maya was born, I was fully prepared to stay at home with her to nurse for as long as possible. But I noticed right away that she was a very different baby from her brother. My son had enjoyed being rocked every night before bed, and nursing the first thing every morning. In contrast, Maya absolutely did not like being rocked. When it was time for bed each evening, rocking only made her fussier. I quickly learned that when she was ready for sleep, the most effective way to calm her was to swaddle her in a blanket and simply lay her in her crib— no rocking, no music ... just quiet.

She also, much to my disappointment, reacted very differently to nursing. Rather than eagerly going after the breast for at least ten minutes on each side like her brother did, she would nurse for about three minutes on one breast and fall asleep. Because she never made it to the second breast, I would often go to bed with one half-full and one completely full breast. When I introduced the bottle to her at three months of age, that was the beginning of the end of breast-feeding. She much preferred the bottle to the breast, and eventually refused the breast altogether in favor of the soy milk bottle.

My disappointment was deep. I had wanted nothing more than to breast-feed for one more year before my lactating years would come to an end, but Maya changed the plan. Between his first marriage and ours, my husband now had four kids and I decided that this would be my last pregnancy. The experts say breast-feeding is the ultimate bond between mother and child, even into the toddler stage. Seeing the breast-feeding phase come to an end was very sad for me. I think I also felt rejected by my sweet little girl.

Maya slept more than most babies, at least from what I had been told. I had planned to stay home from work for at least six months, but by the fourth month I went back to work out of sheer boredom. Maya was sleeping six hours during the day and almost eight hours at night. I felt useless staying home when she didn't really need me to be there.

Our friend Rachel agreed to keep her during the day while John and I worked and my son attended preschool. Rachel seemed like the perfect arrangement because I felt that one-on-one care was the best for an infant. But after a while I began noticing things I wasn't happy with, like Maya being given chocolate at the ripe age of seven months. So when she turned nine months old, I put her in the same preschool her brother attended.

The local Country Day School was one of the top, if not the top, preschools in Tulsa. The school's founder, Marty C., was a well-respected educator who had spent a number of years at the renowned local Episcopal prep school. Marty hired only professionally trained teachers. She based her new school on the most advanced education theories and a strong child-oriented philosophy.

Maya did well in the infant room, and was moved to the toddler room after her first birthday. But by the time she was thirteen months old, her teachers noticed how unhappy she was most days. No longer in cribs, the toddlers took naps on cots and had easy access to one other. It seemed Maya didn't like the constant activity level of the toddler room, and was easily frustrated by all the stimulation. She began to take out her frustration by biting toddlers who pulled her ponytails or got too close to her. She seemed happier when she could find a quiet spot and suck her thumb, but those opportunities were few and far between in a room of twelve toddlers.

She was also easily upset at home. She didn't like being in the kitchen during meal preparation because the clamor of dishes and pots irritated her. When I changed her diaper, she cried when the cold baby wipes touched her bottom, so I had to warm the wipes gently in the microwave before touching her skin. While she seemed to like playing in water, she would also cry when I put her in the bathtub, and cry again when I took her out. Every transition, no matter how gently it was done, was either irritating or painful for her. Getting her dressed and undressed became a huge challenge because she cried when I put her clothes on and cried again when I took them off.

I could feel myself becoming overwhelmed and sad about how she responded to me, and began to question myself as a mother. Was I doing something wrong? Could I do it better? In search for an answer, I began reading books about children with sensitive temperaments, like The Difficult Child. I also wondered if the Vistaril I had taken for nausea during my pregnancy had affected her in any way, and wondered when the drug's effects would wear off. Other than her sensitivity to light, noise, and touch, she seemed perfectly healthy, so I never discussed my sadness and concern with her pediatrician.

After talking with Maya's preschool teachers, John and I decided that preschool just wasn't working, and we placed her in our neighbor's family daycare home. I can't remember exactly how I found Ms. Carol, but she was wonderful. She had four children of her own that she home-schooled. Her kids were ages six through fourteen, and although her home was somewhat busy with activity, it was also quite structured. Besides, I was surprised to learn that the older kids didn't seem to bother Maya. They were doting, attentive, and treated her as one of the family. There was only one other toddler being cared for there, and she and Maya got along just fine. Of course, I got the feeling that Maya stayed in the lap of either Ms. Carol or one of her teenagers all day long, which clearly had advantages over being one of a dozen toddlers fending for themselves in a congested classroom!

Maya's time at Ms. Carol's was a good time. Ms. Carol read to her all the time, and we began to notice an interesting trait. When Maya was about three years old, I went to pick her up one day and Ms. Carol showed me a piece of paper Maya had been writing on that day. Now clearly left-handed, my three-year-old had filled the sheet with row after row of nearly perfect little circles like the letter "O." This pattern of writing seemed extremely unusual for a child her age, especially since other skills, such as language, seemed to be only average for her age. She had met all of her developmental milestones on time: she walked at thirteen months, she spoke in short sentences at about sixteen months, was potty trained at eighteen months. Still, she was not very verbal, and there were times I wondered if her language was on track. A lot of the time, it seemed that she was expressing displeasure, if she expressed anything at all.

With her father's history of hearing impairment and Maya's recurrent ear infections, our pediatrician thought Maya's language might be delayed due to a hearing problem and recommended a full hearing exam by an audiologist. The exam showed a mild hearing impairment and at about eighteen months old, she had surgery to have tubes put in her ears. The tubes allowed fluid to drain off her ears, and we thought it would help her hearing. Even after the surgery though, she wasn't as verbal as other kids her age, and certainly was not as verbal as her brother had been at her age. By contrast, Josh was fully identifying a bird, a cat, a ball, and all sorts of other objects by the time he was eighteen months old. Maya was also different in that she didn't seem very interested in books or educational toys or music. She played alone a lot and sucked her thumb to soothe herself. She was an absolutely gorgeous baby though, and I was so proud of having such beautiful children.

By age four, I became concerned that her lack of regular socializing with other youngsters her age might impair her transition to school, so I placed her back in preschool. This time I chose Trinity Day School, a church-based preschool from which children fed into the local Episcopal Prep School. There was fierce competition for the best preschool slots in town, so I was on a waiting list. Luckily, by the time a slot became available, Maya seemed ready for the classroom experience. She had lots of fun at school, no separation anxiety, and things seemed to go pretty well. She did have some pretty serious temper tantrums, but they seemed fairly normal for her age.

Her attachment to adults at this age, though, was a bit troublesome. She seemed to grab and cling to people she shouldn't, and did not want to be too close to those in her immediate family. Our priest was one person in particular she seemed drawn to. She would cry when she had to leave church, clinging to Reverend Edie as if she were her biological mother. It later occurred to me that perhaps it was Edie's long strawberry blonde braid that Maya was attracted to, so much like the braid of Ms. Carol's daughter, Amy. Although this reasoning might have been off the mark, I could come up with no other explanation for it. Was there something about being around so many people at church that frightened her? But if so, why would she cling to Edie and not me?

At age four, Maya would go into a tantrum that would last five to ten minutes whenever she was told no. I learned to ignore the tantrums and to proceed with getting her into the car or whatever else needed to be done. If I tried to touch her, she would cringe, and she often did not want to be picked up. It made consoling her next to impossible, so I gave up trying and allowed her to calm herself, which sometimes meant listening to crying for a long time. But what else was I supposed to do?

One day she did something that her Dad and I thought she should be punished for. We had told her not to do this over and over again, and she had not obeyed. At first we decided to punish her by stripping her room. So we took all of her stuffed animals and toys out of her room, and had her stay in her room. But after trying this a couple of times, she returned to her previous behavior, so we decided to try another strategy. We rarely spanked our kids, but this time we thought we might need to do so.

So, consistent with the best thinking on parental discipline at the time, we decided to spank her, but used a paddle, rather than a belt or some other more painful method. We took her in her room and swatted her on her bottom once. No reaction. Twice. No reaction. Three times. No reaction. Four times. No reaction. It was clear that we could keep doing this twenty times or more and she would stand there stiff as a brick, and not shed a tear.

Her stubbornness was striking. Neither of us had ever seen a child not react to a spanking. What was going on? We were totally baffled.

Also, somewhere along the line, her sleeping patterns had changed. Perhaps it was around age three or so. All of a sudden, the sleepy baby was no more. Every night she started out in her bed sound asleep after a bedtime story, but awoke during the night and found her way down the hall into our bedroom. We thought it was just a phase she was going through, and let her into our bed. Pretty soon, she was there every night.

After months and months of us getting out of bed in the middle of the night to take her back to hers, we decided our bed was off limits. If she came into our room, she could sleep next to us on the floor but not in the bed with us. We thought this would encourage her to sleep in her own bed, but she continued waking up in the middle of the night and walking to our room at least until age five or so. By then we were using headsets and audiotapes and every other trick we could find to get her to sleep in her own bed. Nothing really worked.

## III. Is Something Wrong with Her?

Over the course of my own childhood, I experienced a lot of different academic settings. I started out as a happy, academically mediocre young girl in the public elementary school within walking distance of my home. There was no such thing as bussing in those days. Schools were still segregated, so all of my classmates were African American and lived close by. Once I got to middle school, I found myself involved in fights, and was often teased and taunted. At the end of eighth grade, my father moved me to a predominantly white Catholic school. I was happier and thrived there academically. That taught me that being in the right school environment could make a huge difference in a child's life chances.

So we decided to stretch ourselves financially and put our kids in the local Episcopal prep school. Maya enrolled in the pre-kindergarten class at age four and a half. The school required an entrance exam to determine appropriate grade placement. I'll never forget the day Maya took her exam. The pre-kindergarten teacher said to me, "I wasn't aware that Maya had a sister. There's no mention of her on your enrollment form."

I looked at her blankly, not quite knowing what to say. After a brief pause, I slowly asked, "A sister?"

She replied, "Yes, Maya told me all about how they play tea-time and play outdoors together."

I said, "Maya doesn't have a sister. She doesn't have any relatives in Oklahoma other than her brother."

The teacher said, "Oh, don't let this worry you. Lots of kids her age have imaginary playmates."

Well, I *was* worried. Maya didn't have a very vivid imagination. And, she wasn't especially expressive either. So I walked away a little embarrassed and wondering whom Maya was talking about. I never asked Maya about it either. Deep down I think I was already noticing that she was different in some way and was afraid to let myself feel my fear that the difference might not be good.

Maya's kindergarten teacher had the reputation for being the best in the school. Maya did well that year, or so it seemed. I never got any bad reports from school, but her final report of kindergarten year concerned me. Among the accolades about what Maya had learned that year, the teacher wrote, "Maya is an explosive, emotionally volatile child." It was stated in somewhat of a casual way, as if to call it to my attention, but not suggest that we needed to fix anything. She was promoted to first grade with the rest of her classmates, and that's when things started to get really shaky.

The first grade teacher was a kind and soft-spoken Native American woman who had also taught my son Josh in first grade. Nancy taught at my church's summer school program and had lots of experience with African American kids.

She revered her Native American heritage and was a docent at the local Native American Museum. She liked my husband and me, and I trusted her implicitly. So when she expressed concern about Maya's volatility, I could no longer push aside my fear of finding something wrong with Maya.

The teacher explained that Maya's days went well except at recess. That was when she would fall apart. According to Nancy, Maya would cry if someone stepped on her toe and drastically over-react to events that were just a normal part of the day. Nancy also had Josh to compare to Maya, and Josh had always done so well at everything he attempted. When she suggested that Maya be evaluated by a child psychologist, I didn't resist this suggestion because it came from someone I knew and respected. Had it come from anyone else, especially a white teacher, I probably would have been angry. Maya was one of only two black kids in a class of twenty-four. It would have been easy for me to think that she was being singled out because of her race. But I couldn't believe that to be true with this teacher, so I followed her advice.

As a public health professional, I was connected to child psychologists and social workers in the Tulsa community, so I knew exactly who to call for a strong recommendation: Sally E. She recommended a woman who agreed to observe my daughter at school. Maya would not know she was being watched. The psychologist would prepare a report and we would discuss the findings with Maya's first grade teacher.

The report came back with only a vague sense of what might be wrong. On one test, Maya was asked to put four pictures together in the correct sequence. The four pictures involved a little girl walking up to a slide, putting her foot on its ladder, climbing to the top, and sliding down. Maya could not figure out the correct sequence of events.

The psychologist also noticed that Maya was especially clingy and that she had trouble separating from me. She thought this might reflect some kind of attachment disorder, and suggested I spend more time with her. I thought she might be right. I had noticed myself pulling away from Maya because she didn't like to be touched. I also remembered how sad I was that she didn't want to breast-feed for very long. Maybe I had withdrawn my attention from her because I felt rejected, and what was happening was my fault. Maybe I needed to find a way to be close to her without touching, I thought. So I started to work at being closer to her but not too close, and that wasn't easy. I felt I was always walking on eggshells around her.

The psychologist also tested her for attention deficit hyperactivity disorder, or ADHD. There was an ADD/ADHD checklist that I had to fill out. If your kid had six or more of the behaviors on the list, that meant she had ADHD or ADD. Maya had only five of the symptoms, so the diagnosis was not firm. The psychologist suggested we try her on Ritalin anyway, and if things got better, we could assume that she had ADHD, and that we should not worry about putting a label on her, as long as the medication was making her better.

It seemed a stretch for me that she might have ADD. She was not hyperactive at home. Josh had been the one to literally do cartwheels across the room, even while someone was talking with him. Maya was far more subdued, except emotionally. If it were possible to be "emotionally hyperactive," she was that. She seemed to over-react to most situations.

I will never forget the first day she was on Ritalin. It was on a Saturday and she and I went to see the movie *Ms. Doubtfire*. Robin Williams was phenomenal, but the story line was one I thought many first graders would find challenging to follow. I wondered if she was getting it. About midway through the movie, she began to ask extremely insightful questions such as, "Why can't Ms. Doubtfire just be herself?" She also observed how sad Ms. Doubtfire must be that she couldn't be at home with her kids anymore.

Since Maya had never appeared to be observant or articulate about people, and even seemed unable to comprehend the simplest social situations, I was totally blown away. Was this the effect that the Ritalin was supposed to have? It was so obvious that this medication was having a strong, positive effect on her brain. That little white pill had given me a completely different child—engaged, present, and expressive. I liked what I was seeing, and was relieved that maybe I could let go of the concerns about her, and that maybe it wasn't my fault after all.

# IV. Perfect Angel, Pure Anger

At the end of first grade, John's job transferred him to Detroit. Moving across the country to a place we had never been was a really big deal. We were all excited about the new adventure, although we had to leave our wonderful, brand new, two-story home that we had built just two years before.

Detroit was Motown, rich with culture and diversity and the automotive capital of the world. Right across the Detroit River was Canada—another country! As we studied the options for schools and neighborhoods, we saw the many lakes on the maps of Detroit suburbs. We loved water, and had always had a creek or a pond near where we lived. The suburban Detroit neighborhoods also had some of the best public schools, so we knew where we would settle. After two house-hunting trips to Michigan, we found an expensive but small home in the neighborhood and school district that we wanted. At least we wouldn't have to pay for private school anymore. We could write off mortgage interest but not private school tuition, so our decision was made.

The schools in Michigan stayed in session at least three weeks longer than Oklahoma schools, so the kids were able to attend their last weeks of first and fourth grades in Michigan. This worked out perfectly because they got to meet kids as soon as we moved there and had playmates over the summer. The homes in the neighborhood were on big lots and the streets were perfect for riding bikes. The first summer was a good one.

Second grade for Maya was uneventful, except for the day she saved her teacher's life. That's a little bit of an exaggeration, but it was an unforgettable day nonetheless. During class time, Maya's teacher fainted and it was Maya who darted to the front office for help. She did well academically, and had a friend or two that she liked spending time with. Although she still needed the Ritalin, her behavior was acceptable at home and in the classroom.

Maya participated in some of the same activities she had enjoyed in Tulsa, like dance school. She also learned to ice skate, and took lessons on the weekend. Although she was in the third grade by now, she would still cling to me when I took her to practice. She didn't seem to like crowds, and Saturdays at the skating rink were packed with eager kids running and jumping around on their ice skates. Other kids were curious and excited—Maya was quiet and anxious.

She insisted that I be there to pick her up the minute skating class was over, and that I not be late. It was as if she wouldn't know what to do with herself if she had to be alone, even for a few minutes. I began to see fearfulness and anxiety in her for the first time.

She also played softball at school and soccer during the summer, but she wasn't very good at either sport. She never seemed to be able to figure out how the games worked. She would do as she was told, but long after others had figured out the game, she remained confused. After many attempts to involve her in team sports, we eventually gave up and stuck with ice-skating for a number of years.

She also didn't seem very interested in extracurricular activities at school. It troubled me that she still didn't have many friends, and didn't participate in any of the activities that interested other kids her age. When she decided to participate in the math pentathlon at school in fourth grade, we were thrilled. But when she didn't win as often as she would have liked, she took the losses pretty badly, and wanted to throw in the towel.

When the math penthalon came around the next year, she agreed to participate, but was pretty unenthusiastic about it. She just wasn't excelling in things she tried, although she seemed to have the intellectual ability. Maya did have a few challenges academically, but nothing severe. For example, she didn't read as quickly or as well as other fourth graders, so we enrolled her in a summer reading camp. The camp used memorization and dramatic acting to improve reading skills, and it really did help her. Afterward, she seemed on par with her peers, although she tended to transpose letters on some words pronouncing "saw" as "was," for example. But over time this seemed to disappear.

By fourth grade, around the age of nine, social problems were beginning to emerge. She and her Dad didn't get along well sometimes, but their relationship seemed to be deteriorating. She was also getting along poorly with kids at school, so I enrolled her in a group therapy class where kids her age learned to deal with their anger. She hated group therapy. She thought the other kids were dumb and that she didn't belong there. By then, her father and I were also talking divorce.

This nice, upscale elementary school in suburban Detroit rarely had fights. So, who was this angry child anyway? Was this the same bright and cheerful daughter who had been selected to read the "I Have a Dream" speech over the school's PA system on Martin Luther King Jr.'s birthday that year? It was the only school in the district with a black principal—Ms. B. I knew Ms. B. took a special interest in Maya, so I always felt she was being nurtured there. But when Ms. B. called to tell me Maya had punched her fourth-grade classmate, I was embarrassed and disappointed.

Her Dad also had a reputation for being stubborn and volatile as a kid. In fact, his teenage friends had nicknamed him "TT" for "Temper Tantrum," something I was unaware of until after our divorce. Now he was coming home each day with his anger, rigidity, and unreasonable expectations. I had lived with this to a greater or lesser extent for more than fifteen years, and finally I had enough. Later, I recalled something else as well.

Back in 1994, our lives had been filled with excitement and change when my husband was granted his request to transfer to Detroit. Our time in Oklahoma had been quiet and simple, but my husband and I yearned for more—more career opportunity, greater access to things we enjoyed like jazz, and a faster pace. Several special people in our lives had left Tulsa, also seeking more of what life had to offer.

As we prepared for the cross-country move, my husband came home to Oklahoma in early May to help with the packing. But unlike his usual high-energy self, instead of helping with all that needed to be done, he literally sat on the sofa all week. Somehow, with all the activity going on around him, he could not move. I found it strange, but I never really discussed it with him. Instead I assumed that he was just tired from all of the transition in our lives. It wasn't until later that I realized that this may have been the first sign of a more serious problem and that it could have implications for some of Maya's behaviors.

In our new home, after the divorce, I told Maya the move would give her a chance to start over, to reclaim her reputation as a bright, cheerful, and compassionate student. We could leave the embarrassment of elementary school behavior behind us and start anew.

The new job I had been offered was one I could only have dreamed of—joining the management team in an organization devoted to providing free health care for poor children. The salary and benefits were great, and I would be able to prove to my ex-husband that I could not only make it on my own, but would do better without him. He had tried so hard to bring me down—even told me straight out that he wanted to "break" me, as if I were a horse. No one had ever said anything more painful to me. And no matter what, I was determined that the divorce and the move to a new city would be a step forward, not a step back.

# V. Calm Before the Storm

The kids didn't seem to mind the move at all. It was a perfect time. Josh was entering high school and Maya middle school, so even if we had stayed in our old neighborhood, they both would have been attending new schools in the fall anyway. And of course I had carefully planned it this way, to try to minimize the trauma of the divorce on them. After all, I plan *everything*.

Josh clearly missed his Dad. His face looked so sad the day we told him about the divorce. But I assured both kids that they would spend every other weekend with Dad, who was now only an hour away. I would even drive them halfway there to make it easier on Dad, and to show that I had no desire to keep them from each other.

Feeling sure that he would see his Dad regularly, Josh was happy to be around more black kids than our previous neighborhood had allowed, and as soon as he located the baseball and football fields, he was good to go! He settled right in, making friends quickly—but then again, he'd always been so adaptable and easy going.

And he loved the new house! It was so big and so much newer than our last home. Choosing the right school for him was a no-brainer; he would attend the high school less than a mile from home. I had been deliberate about choosing a nice, upscale neighborhood, and the community high school was considered one of the better ones in town. As is usually the case, the suburban schools were believed to be superior, but I refused to put my kids in another setting where they might be the only black kids in class.

Maya was also excited to be moving away, but for her, the school environment would have to be carefully chosen. Although she was smart, she required more personal attention to manage her ADHD, and to stay organized and on top of assignments. She seemed to become overwhelmed and over-stimulated in large groups, so she would need a small school and a small class size. It was important to let her choose, so we began to visit schools. All the while I hoped she would like the small Lutheran school I had in mind, but I had to let her decide.

Her choice reflected that she had good instincts about what she needed. Our visit to the public middle school in the neighborhood was fine—lots of black kids and a nice facility. The teachers seemed reasonably attentive to her during our visit, but the school was a large maze, a bit overcrowded, and easy to get lost in. But the Lutheran school was tiny by comparison, with only one classroom per grade. The total enrollment was about two hundred, grades kindergarten through eighth. The entire school consisted of two long hallways and two levels—that was it. Kindergarten through grade five downstairs, and grades six to eight upstairs. The school had the requisite cafeteria and gym, a nice playground and was about 50 percent African American! Other than that, no bells or whistles. The sanctuary was next door to the school, connected by a short hallway. Going to school really meant going to church, too.

And the teachers were so kind, making us feel very welcome from the moment we entered the building. The tuition was reasonable and there was even an after school program until 6 p.m. every day. When we left the building after our tour, Maya said, "I think I want to go here. The people are so nice, and I wouldn't want to disappoint them by going somewhere else!"

Maya's sleeping problems re-emerged. I also noticed that her sleep had a different quality about it. It seemed she was actually sleepwalking now, unable to awaken although she was moving through the house from her room to my room. She continued to come into my room at night throughout middle school. But sleepwalking was a very mild aberration compared to the other things that began to happen.

When Maya was nine years old, I tried to have conversations with her about menstruation and sexuality. I started my periods at age nine, so I wanted her to be prepared. She was also starting to develop breast tissue, although the Ritalin suppressed her appetite and she was thin as a rail. But whenever I approached the subject, she frowned in disgust and wasn't interested. Even after she started her period at age ten, she would not discuss it with me and insisted that the whole matter was her secret, which is why the next series of events was totally unexpected.

# VI. The REAL Drama Begins

Maya was eleven years old when we moved to Flint in the summer of 1998. The move was both victory and escape. Leaving an unhappy marriage where I felt lonely and sad most of the time was clearly a step towards regaining my sanity, although I was consumed by grief over the loss of an intact family. My parents divorced when I was fourteen, and I began counting the divorces that kept happening around me. I also knew the statistics showed black families as broken and dysfunctional. But not only was I unhappy, I hated witnessing my kids being yelled at and humiliated by their father. I thought that a "good" mother would do what she could to protect her children from such treatment. So I not only decided to divorce, I also moved far enough away from their Dad to be safe, but not too far that the kids couldn't see him.

For me, it was a personal safety issue too. My ex-husband was an abusive man. He never hit me, but he was a bully. When he sensed I wanted to leave him, he brought his .38-caliber pistol out of the basement and conveniently placed it on the nightstand next to our bed. He knew I hated guns and I knew there was no other reason for him to do this but to intimidate me. The night I was packing to leave, he came into the house and kicked in the door to my daughter's bedroom, where she and I were putting her things into boxes. I decided to call my friends Steve and Marcia to come over and sit with me while I packed. Always concerned with appearances, their presence calmed him down enough to let me get out of the house. As I drove my Jeep away, I thanked God that I had safely escaped.

I remember the day my husband and I told the kids we were divorcing. Josh looked sadder than I had ever seen him, was very quiet afterwards, and really didn't want to talk about it. Like most boys, he kept his feelings to himself although he must have felt the tension and anger in the house. Maya's response was quite different. She told her fifth-grade teacher that the divorce was a victory, since she felt that both she and I were being mistreated.

I never quite figured out why Maya was treated with an iron hand by her father, while her brother and half-brothers enjoyed a relatively friendly relationship with him. The difference was so striking that Maya always noticed it and, as any young child would, felt sad and angry about it. Was it her passion, independence, and defiance that rubbed her father the wrong way? Or was it the chauvinist values of submission that some men expect of their wives and daughters, while granting their sons full rein of the house, the neighborhood, and the world? Was this simply a result of his belief in male privilege?

Things got worse for Maya in Flint, much worse. And they got worse right away. I was anxious for the kids to make new friends in the new neighborhood. Maya spent hours riding her bike and house-hopping that first summer. I never gave any thought to the possibility that the neighborhood could be an unsafe place. We were in a beautiful, upper-middle class suburb, wonderfully racially diverse. Yet it seems it was only weeks before nasty rumors about Maya began to surface. I dismissed them as being the cruel behavior of silly kids who had it in for the new kid on the block. But over time, the rumors increased. Josh was heartsick as he told about the stories he was hearing from other boys—stories of sexual activity by his eleven-year-old sister, who only months prior was repulsed at any mention of sex.

Luckily, since Maya didn't attend the neighborhood school, the rumors never reached the door of her small Lutheran school. Even though Maya had chosen the school, I too had agreed that this might be the perfect academic setting for her, where she would get the individual attention she needed to succeed. It was a tough school to enter in sixth grade, though. Most of the students had been attending the school since kindergarten. This meant that the girlie cliques had already been formed, and they weren't eager to open up to Maya. Although she played basketball and volleyball, and continued her dance lessons outside of school, she still didn't have a best girlfriend. Her best friend was a very nice boy in the neighborhood, Phillip, who she no doubt confided in and who always loved and accepted her.

Since the divorce, the kids' father would drive halfway to our meeting spot (about a thirty-minute drive for each of us) to pick them up every other weekend. They seemed to enjoy visiting with him, at least for a while. Before long, they were both too busy with their social lives of sports and school events, and started to prefer staying at home on the weekends.

Meanwhile, Maya's behavior seemed to become more and more unusual. She seemed to be somewhat out of control, but it was hard to pinpoint what was going on. She was always on the telephone, like most teens, but her love affair with the phone seemed to have a driven quality to it. It seemed she couldn't go five minutes without calling someone, no matter the time of day. She called one boy so often that his parents called to ask me to curtail her phone calls. Literally, the minute she ended one call, she would dial another number. Then there was the sleepwalking and talking in her sleep. Always, she made her way to my bed.

It was almost a year after the incident that I learned she had pierced her own belly button. The discovery happened very matter-of-factly, as I overheard her telling her cousin. I was so shocked I was numb. I couldn't imagine someone doing that. I consulted the psychiatrist again, and I must have told her that I thought something more than ADHD was going on with her. I remember her saying, "If you want me to try a mood stabilizer, I will." The tone in which she said it didn't have enough conviction for me. It was as if she was uncertain the mood stabilizer was needed. So I backed off and decided to wait before making another med change.

Then one day when she had just completed the sixth grade, I got a call from a neighbor that she had seen two boys enter my home after school that day. When I arrived home and asked Maya about it, she casually admitted that the two boys had been there, and that she had sex with both of them, each while the other watched.

"Did they use condoms?" I asked.

She said, "Yes." In my disbelief that this could be happening, I asked her to show me the condoms. Maya walked out of the room and came back with a cookie can. I looked inside the can and saw the used condoms. As I realized her account of what had transpired was real, I became nauseous with terror.

I knew that many kids began having sex at early ages, but twelve years old just seemed totally beyond belief, especially for a child of mine! What shocked me even more was that more than one boy was involved and she had no remorse or shame about it. She had no love relationship with these boys. It was as casual as two kids sneaking a smoke behind the barn. It was not only what she had done, but the way she talked about it that let me know that my child's judgment was terribly impaired and that she might be mentally ill. I called the homes of both boys, one of whose parents I knew. That same night, in my living room, all of the parents had a serious conversation with each other and with the youth, but I wasn't sure at the end of it all if Maya really understood the magnitude of what she had done. The next day I took her to Planned Parenthood for an examination for sexually transmitted diseases and a prescription for birth control pills.

Events continued to spiral downward in seventh grade. Maya seemed angry so much of the time, so I re-enrolled her in therapy, this time an anger management class. Before the social worker would accept her, she conducted a psychological evaluation and concluded that Maya had obsessive-compulsive disorder (OCD) and oppositional defiant disorder (ODD). She also said that Maya had revealed something during the diagnostic consultation that I should know. With Maya's permission, the social worker revealed that Maya had been either coerced or forced to have sex with a neighborhood boy during the summer we moved to Flint. She was just entering the sixth grade at the time, and was only eleven years old. I recalled the rumors that flew that first summer in Flint.

The social worker thought that this incident might not only be connected to Maya's anger, but also to her increased sexual behavior. It all seemed reasonable—a young girl violated by an older guy later becomes promiscuous. I'd read often enough about sexually abused girls and how they often become sex workers, runaways, troubled in many ways. Could that explain the bizarre behavior I'd seen over the past two years?

Driving home from one of her anger management classes, I explained that the boys had taken advantage of her and that what happened wasn't her fault. I asked if she felt she had a choice in the matter. Maya said no, but she also said that she had wanted to do it. I couldn't make sense of what she said. Those two responses seemed contradictory to me.

A major part of the challenge with a child like Maya was that not only did she have problems regulating her moods, but she also had a clear and persistent diagnosis of attention deficit hyperactivity disorder (ADHD). It was hard for me to determine whether she was angry and frustrated because of things that were going on in her life, like our divorce and our move to a new community, or whether her anger was a symptom of the frustration she experienced with her ADHD. Did she need counseling for some trauma she had experienced, or did her brain just need the drugs for her ADHD? It was all so complex and confusing. Having a background in psychology and public health was both a blessing and a curse. My training had helped me know something wasn't right. But my training certainly wasn't enough to help me know what was really going on or what to do about it.

It also didn't help that there was so much controversy in the news and in the medical and educational professions about whether ADD and ADHD were true mental disorders, or whether the educational system, frustrated by overcrowded classrooms and dwindling resources, were medicating kids who were essentially healthy just to manage their behavior. And after all, Maya's diagnosis in first grade of borderline, rather than full ADHD, was because she didn't fully meet the criteria for ADHD at that time. When the doctor prescribed Ritalin, it was done with the attitude of, "Let's try this to see if it helps. If it helps, then she probably has ADHD. If it doesn't help, she must not have it."

The Ritalin did work, in a major way. It seemed to unscramble her brain and allow her to connect the dots between events and consequences. She became more verbal and more articulate, and her comprehension improved. But by the time she reached puberty, problems reemerged and the doctors felt that maybe she had developed a tolerance to the Ritalin and that it was time to switch to another ADHD drug. She was prescribed Concerta, which she took for a month or so.

When she started Concerta in sixth grade, she totally wigged out. Her behavior was so unusual—not particularly aggressive or depressed—just very different, as if she had lost her ability to be logical or exercise judgment. So, her doctor took her off Concerta and switched to Adderall, which for her became sort of a miracle drug. She became calmer and more focused, and better able to complete tasks she had started. The doctor also prescribed Zoloft to treat her anger and irritability.

In retrospect, I think the Zoloft caused her to be more irritable and depressed, and even suicidal. Middle school is a hard time for most kids. It was really hard time for me as a kid, so when Maya started to talk about killing herself, I didn't think she was serious about it, and I didn't panic. I even thought she was being manipulative and overly dramatic, a "drama queen" as such females are called. But she also had become overly interested in sex and had tried alcohol and marijuana. She hid a lot of her behavior from me, and in some cases it was months or years before I discovered some of the behaviors. She also became quite agitated at times, which I learned later happened mostly when she smoked marijuana.

I came to work each day depressed and embattled. My boss and my closest co-workers could see my distress. When I was offered the opportunity to work for my company's affiliate as a consultant rather than a forty-hour week, I jumped at the chance. To this day, I credit my employer with helping me save my child.

Despite working from home and being fully available to Maya, eighth grade was no better. Her teachers said she was brilliant, but her grades were only mediocre. I decided to get another psychological evaluation and educational assessment, and landed upon the best psychologist we had ever had. Dr. Max Taylor diagnosed her with ADHD and impulse control disorder, and said he saw little evidence of OCD and ODD. He also said she had an IQ in the superior range. He agreed to counsel her, and the psychiatrist in his practice, Dr. Audrey Hill, would prescribe medications.

One day I was called to the school because Maya was having problems breathing. It was Grandparents Day, and the classroom had been filled with older adults visiting the school. That morning, Maya had expressed sadness that her grandparents weren't there, and asked who would be there for her? Something happened that added to her frustration, and unknown to her teacher, Maya decided to hold her breath because she didn't want to live anymore. When her fingertips lost color, the school thought she might be having an asthma attack and called me. I rushed over to the school, looked her over, and immediately could see that she was having no trouble breathing. I managed to calmly get her to the car where she confessed to holding her breath so she would die. I called her psychologist and he suggested taking her to the ER, which I did. By the time we arrived at the ER, she was completely calm. The doctors and nurses looked her over and released her. I don't think I ever mentioned to them that she had intentionally tried to harm herself, and I'm not sure why I didn't. Instead, I made an appointment with her psychologist who agreed to see her a few days later.

Dr. Taylor was the first professional to tell me about Section 504 of the Americans with Disabilities Act. He recommended that I remove her from private school and enroll her in a public school because by law, they would be required to provide her with educational accommodations. It wasn't long before I had no other choice.

In the spring of eighth grade, Maya was permanently expelled from school for making a threatening gesture with an Exacto knife. Her school had a zero tolerance policy for violence, so neither threats nor actual incidents of violence were tolerated. Since putting her in the under-funded Flint Public Schools was not an acceptable option in my mind, I decided to move back to her old school district, which was one of the best in the state, if not the nation. Since I could work from home no matter where I lived, there was nothing to hold me back. I didn't bother to try to sell my house at the time; the main thing was to get her in a quality public school as soon as possible. I wanted her to have a clean start, without any stigma or pre-judgment. So, here we were, on the move again. I told Maya that this would be the last time we would move because of her behavior. My former boss had once told me of the witty saying, "Wherever I go, there I am." It was a clever way of saying that you can't run away from a problem if you are the problem. I tried to get Maya to see that her behavior was creating the circumstances in which she was living. Despite my teaching, she has trouble grasping that concept even today.

# VII. Why Does This Keep Happening?

So here we were, back in our old Birmingham neighborhood, fifty miles away from Flint. We left our beautiful 2,800-square foot home unoccupied, and found an apartment to rent—a large one-bedroom for the three of us. This upscale school district was short on apartments to rent, so only one-bedrooms were available. Maya and I slept together in the bedroom, and Josh slept on the sleep sofa in the living room. At least the apartment was right down the street from the high school Josh would be attending.

Paying a mortgage on a house we no longer lived in, plus rent on a tiny apartment was no joke. But staying in Flint was not an option. The public schools there wouldn't know what to do with her and the private school had kicked her out. Birmingham had some of the best public schools in the country. I chose not to tell them that Maya had been expelled from a private school in Flint.

When we moved back, Maya had only a month or two of middle school left. My son had wanted to get back to his old district in time to play baseball that season, so we didn't wait until the school year ended. Besides, Maya had been told she couldn't come back to the little Lutheran school, so we really didn't have a choice but to move immediately.

I began keeping a journal somewhere along the way, to try to make sense of all the crazy things that were happening to me. I had kept journals since I was in elementary school, but since becoming an adult, I only journaled when I was troubled. And I surely was troubled now.

*Journal entry: May 25, 2001, 2:50 p.m.*

*We've only been in this new middle school now for a month or so. But today, Mr. S. calls me and says Maya cannot come back to school on Tuesday because he has evidence that she developed a "hit list" of fifteen to eighteen kids that she intended to harm.*

*According to Mr. S., on Wednesday he received a call from an emotionally distraught parent about this "hit list" and wanted to know if his/her child was in danger. Then a second parent called him about a list of kids who were to be beaten up. Then the teacher in an art class says something about this list. Supposedly, Maya had "dropped the list" outside of her locker. Someone then went to the copy machine and ran copies of the list, so 80 to 90 percent of the eighth graders now have it. And then a third parent called and asked if it were safe for her child to come back to school.*

*Public Laws 101, 102, and 103 state that written or verbal threats can lead to expulsion. When I spoke with Maya about his, she said that she and a classmate had identified a list of people she would try to become friends with in the future. The classmate suggested that Maya should try to acknowledge the various accomplishments of these people and be more pleasant towards them. All of this because Maya still had no friends.*

*I called the classmate's Dad, and he and his daughter completely corroborated the story. I then called Detective Miller, one of the school police liaisons. When I started to cry, he asked if I was getting angry with him. I explained that Mr. S. had called, left a message that Maya couldn't come back to school on Tuesday, couldn't go on the end of school field trip to Cedar Point, and then took off for the weekend. He wasn't at all sympathetic.*

On Tuesday I called Mr. S. and told him my understanding of what had happened: that Maya had a difficult time making friends at Berkshire (the new school), that she and her classmate put together a list of kids Maya would work to be friends with, and that someone else had taken the list, added "Hit List" at the top of it, and distributed it.

The following Wednesday, we met at the school at 7:40 a.m. I had asked Maya's father to join me. Mr. S. had interviewed the top suspects, and talked to the classmate, who said she thought someone else had done this. He worked with the English teachers to obtain handwriting samples of the top suspects, and agreed that the list may have been altered.

Mr. S. indicated that there would be major consequences for the kids who altered the list. Maya's father couldn't believe we were sitting at the school having this discussion. Weeping, he told Mr. S. that there was no way his daughter would have done such a thing. But John was so removed from the day-to-day drama that Maya created, he didn't realize what she was really capable of, and I had never told him what happened at the Lutheran school in Flint.

Mr. S. called the four parents to let them know that Maya had been "exonerated." I was so relieved; but still, what a nightmare this had been. Why do things like this keep happening? What on earth is wrong?

I was beginning to notice a pattern, though. It seemed that the week before Maya's period was always the most challenging time for her. There would be anger and sadness and irritability. There would be conflicts at school and at home. When she crumpled on the floor of our tiny apartment and cried the week before her period when she was a freshman in high school, I knew there had to be a way to get her some relief. I just didn't know how.

# VIII. The Hardest Part

Probably the hardest part of the continuous struggles to manage Maya's illness was doing it all alone. Although we were now back in the community where Maya's father lived, he still chose to have very little to do with her. Oh, he came to all the special events—her cheerleading games, her freshmen play, her choir's performances. But every morning I was the one who struggled to get her out of bed, who sat with her on the edge of that bed and cried with her because she didn't want to go to school, who watched her slump on the floor after school, a crumple of tears because she had ruined a relationship with someone at school and felt she had no friends. I was the one who lived through these painful every days with her. I was always drained, and either numb or sad, wondering where I would get the energy to stay focused enough to figure out what she needed and how I could get it for her.

Once I was so desperate for a break that I sent her to Houston to visit her half-brother JJ who was in his late twenties. She must have been about fourteen years old, and by now had a colorful sexual history. Only a couple of days after she had been there, JJ called to tell me she would have to come back home, that he couldn't handle her. She had argued and gotten into fights with his ten-year-old adopted son, his household was no longer peaceful, and he was sending her home. Perhaps I was expecting too much, but he barely offered to help her in any way; his main concern was getting her—his fourteen-year-old sister, not some stranger off the street—out of his house.

He also told me how in the mall, Maya would walk up to young boys she didn't know, strike up a conversation, and give them her phone number. He and his wife were appalled by this.

That night Maya told me over the phone that she couldn't get sexual images out of her head, that all she could think about was having sex. It made me so very sad to hear my daughter, who was so young and pretty, thinking of expressing her sexuality so indiscriminately and at such a tender age.

The next day, as JJ requested, I changed her airline ticket and she came home after only four of the seven days I so desperately needed away from her just to regain strength to continue.

My sister knew all about Maya's challenges and had been a trusted and non-judgmental confidante for me through my divorce and early years as a single parent. If anyone understood what Maya and I were going through, my sister did. So a year or so later when I asked if Maya could come to visit her, I was hurt by her answer. She didn't think her husband and Maya would get along. He was a strict disciplinarian, and he wasn't especially understanding towards his own kids who were pretty well behaved, let alone a kid like Maya.

I wondered why my sister never stood up to him. There was nothing docile about her; in fact, she didn't skip a beat explaining to me why Maya couldn't come to visit. Growing up, she never held her tongue when there was something to fuss about. And although I was the one more likely to hold my tongue in those days, had the situation been reversed, I would have welcomed my niece into our home. After all, didn't she know how desperate I was for help? But now, years later, I know that her decision to not bring Maya into a setting where she wouldn't be accepted was absolutely the best thing.

And then there were the "too helpful" relatives, like my brother and his wife. They both felt Maya just needed to be controlled, sort of like an animal in the wild. It seemed to them that all Maya's problems were the result of poor parenting on my part. Her father, by the way, was absolved of any responsibility for parenting her. Any time she acted out, the responsibility, or lack thereof, was placed solely on me.

Needless to say, since everyone declined to let Maya come visit, there I was again, all on my own, raising this troubled and erratic child I gave birth to, nursed at my breast, and cried with on school mornings. She was all mine, and I was all alone. That was the hardest part.

# IX. We Go It Alone

Although I had so many reasons to give up on ever getting Maya the help she needed, I never did. So, after we moved back to Birmingham, I found yet another counselor for Maya, a young woman whom Maya liked very much and was actually willing to accept as a therapist.

This new therapist, Darlene, was never controlling or judgmental, just helpful in offering insights and ways of managing Maya's behavior and emotions. She helped Maya see the consequences of her behavior and learn to take responsibility for her actions. Things went very well with Darlene for a while, and I finally felt I had some support. Darlene never condemned my parenting or blamed me for Maya's behavior. She was steady in her love and kindness, an approach that both Maya and I really needed.

Maya began her freshmen year in high school on a fairly positive note, but after a month or so, started to be involved in a lot of peer conflicts. It seemed that every other week I was being called to the school about some conflict or altercation involving Maya.

Her brother was affected by all of this too. About a semester into her freshmen year, Josh, who was now a senior, punched a guy for saying something derogatory about his sister. Josh was not the kind of kid to fight, but he would not hesitate to defend himself or his family. So when this happened, I knew that there was more going on with her at school than I knew about.

Maya enjoyed acting, and attended several acting camps just prior to entering high school. During that first semester of her freshmen year, she tried out for the school play *Brigadoon*, and got a nice singing and dancing part. Things went pretty well with that, with only one sort of unusual event. That was when a girl at rehearsal practice went into a coughing spell, and Maya called 911. Her overreaction to this event was obvious to everyone but her.

About a month or two into the second semester of her freshmen year, I got a call from the ninth-grade dean, who said very sensitively that he was spending an excessive amount of time mediating conflicts involving Maya and that he couldn't devote so much of his time to one student. He recommended that Maya be evaluated for "special services" at the high school. That was the beginning of a life-saving journey for her and for me.

After being evaluated by the school psychologist, Maya was certified as emotionally impaired, and recommended for special education, despite her very high IQ. I was shocked and amazed to learn that this high school, located in this very wealthy suburb of Detroit, had a plethora of supports for kids like Maya. A multidisciplinary team of five people was formed for her: 1) the academic counselor, 2) the school social worker, 3) the ninth-grade dean, 4) the school psychologist, and 5) the head of the Special Ed department. The team called Maya's father and me in to meet with them and prepare an IEP (individualized education plan). Beginning immediately, Maya would attend the Learning Resource Center (LRC) for an hour each day, be given extra time to complete assignments, be allowed to have "time outs" with a pass to leave class whenever things got emotionally charged for her. Each of her teachers would be required to submit Maya's weekly progress reports to the Learning Resource Center teacher.

This team was prepared to do whatever was needed to help Maya succeed. I was so happy to get some real help and support for her. Although Maya may not have been able to appreciate what this support would mean for her future, it was clear to me that after several emotionally draining and physically exhausting years, a burden was finally being lifted from my shoulders.

Maya did pretty well with the support. The Learning Resource Center was perfect for her. I never had to worry about her doing homework, losing assignments, or when she should be studying for an exam. The LRC teacher, Carol G., took care of all that.

My first and only bump with the LRC came soon after Maya started attending the center. Observing Maya's uneven performance—good some days, not so good on others—the LRC teacher said she thought that Maya might be bipolar. I looked at her in shock. I thought to myself, "You've only known my child for a week and you are already labeling her?" I was really angry with her, but said nothing. She went on to say that her daughter was bipolar, and then a light bulb went off within me. Oh, I thought, just because your daughter is bipolar, you think every kid that has challenges must have the same problem. I really resented her for diagnosing Maya. After all, she wasn't a psychologist or therapist. She was just another teacher like the rest of them. It wasn't until a year or more later that I realized that when someone is the parent of an emotionally impaired child—living with them, struggling with them, and worrying about them day in and day out—they know more about mental illness than all the psychologists and psychiatrists combined!

Maya had also tried out for the cheerleading team at the beginning of her freshmen year, and made it! It was another success in her history of so many failures, despite being extremely bright, pretty, and at times even lovable. However, her success with cheerleading was short-lived. Maya just didn't get along with girls her age. She began to get into conflicts with girls on the team. As a flyer, Maya was dependent on these girls to catch her when she was thrown into the air during a cheer. One day, one of the girls rather conveniently missed her spotting, and Maya crashed to the floor, hitting her head on the hard tile surface of the high school hallway. The coach called me, and I rushed her to the emergency room with facial paralysis and a severe headache.

By the grace of God, the CT scan revealed no brain hemorrhage, but Maya lost short-term memory and her ability to do math for several weeks. Of course, cheerleading was put on hold, and it was later suggested by her coach that Maya might have been dropped on purpose.

I recall having similar experiences in high school—mean girls ganging up on me, telling malicious lies, betraying my trust. When we spoke to her counselor about it, she gave Maya an article to read about mean girls and why they do the things they do. Like me, Maya never had any compassion or sympathy for them.

The next semester, at the beginning of her sophomore year, Maya went out for the cheerleading team again, and again was successful. However, early in the school year, Maya blurted out a profanity during one game, while cheering during halftime. She was kicked off the team. My heart ached for her as she cried in disappointment at being let go. She had tried so hard to be a good member of the team, but it was as though she had no control over her behavior and what came out of her mouth. She felt such remorse afterwards. She cried and cried. And I cried with her. I knew that the coach had to take disciplinary action against Maya. The coach was even sad to have to do it. I was embarrassed by Maya's behavior, but at the same time I knew that something was really wrong with my child. She loved cheering and would never intentionally jeopardize her spot on the team. What I didn't realize at the time was that she was having a manic episode. To a novice, her behavior wasn't mania—it was just a kid acting out.

Separated from the cheerleading squad for a second time, she fell into despondency. She didn't have a lot to do with her free time, and the lack of having structure in the after school hours became a problem. Bored, she told me she wanted to get her navel pierced again. Having learned over the years that if I said no she would do what she wanted anyway, I decided to take her to a place that had been recommended because the piercings were done by a trained nurse and the needles were always clean.

This same place, though, was in a little mall with a head shop and an incense store. Unknown to me, Maya started to spend more and more time there. I had never participated in the drug scene and did not recognize the signs of trouble. Months later when she was suspended from school for being in possession of pipes and other drug paraphernalia, it was clear that she had developed more than an occasional relationship with marijuana.

She was suspended for several days. Again, the school was more supportive of her than it had to be. There was a zero tolerance policy on drug use, but because we agreed to drug counseling, Maya would only be suspended rather than permanently expelled.

Still, her drug use was out in the open and that meant the end of our relationship with Darlene. Maya's substance use meant she needed a different kind of therapy, according to Darlene, and a different therapist—one who specialized in substance abuse. So, after years of searching for, and finally finding a therapist that Maya really liked and would commit to working with, she had blown it. Again.

We saw the recommended substance abuse counselor once. This thin, wiry woman looked so haggard and gaunt I wondered if she had an eating disorder. She didn't look whole or happy. I wondered how such a person could help Maya. Perhaps she was a recovering addict and that was her source of expertise. But I did not trust her with my daughter.

Also, I believed that Maya's substance abuse was a symptom of another problem. I didn't want to treat the symptom—I wanted clarity about the root problem.

Meanwhile, Josh graduated from high school and enrolled at Duke University. Once he left for school and our apartment lease was up, I began to search for a larger apartment. I found a two-bedroom a little farther away from Maya's high school. As she was getting older and I was becoming more fatigued, I really needed her to have her own bedroom.

Since Darlene wouldn't see us anymore, I called my former therapist in Flint (who I had stopped seeing because I believed him to be a racist, but whom I otherwise respected), and asked for a recommendation for a new therapist for Maya. He sent us to an upscale mental health practice very near our new apartment in Birmingham. In fact, it was practically walking distance away. Even though the particular therapist he sent us to was not accepting new patients, we were able to see another person in that same practice, a well-put-together, forty-ish Jewish woman who had an air of authority about her. Maya didn't like her, probably because, unlike her other therapist who smiled and communicated love and concern for Maya, this woman was no-nonsense and not very warm. She communicated that she knew what was best for you, and that she was good at "summing you up."

Maya grudgingly went to see her, but after a while, refused to go. I continued to see this new therapist without Maya for a while, by now desperately needing help in knowing how to parent her. The older she got, the more difficult it was to control her. Although the therapist did help me somewhat, I never really developed a strong fondness for her, nor a real deep connection. Perhaps the best thing that came out of being at the Birmingham clinic was finding Dr. L.

Dr. L. was the psychiatrist on staff. Maya was still taking Adderall and Zoloft, and by now had also been prescribed Buspar, which wasn't having much of an effect. She seemed to be a bit more irritable in some ways. Putting her on birth control pills had helped, although Dr. L. never really responded to my observation that she was worse during the premenstrual week. About five or six months after beginning therapy at the new clinic, and seeing Dr. L. for refills of Adderall and Zoloft, Maya's behavior began to escalate.

When Dr. L. learned she had continued to smoke marijuana, he threatened to stop prescribing Adderall to her. Of all the medications she had taken over the years—Ritalin, Zoloft, Concerta, Buspar—Adderall was her favorite. With Adderall she could pay attention in class and stay awake in the afternoons. Without it, she couldn't figure out what to do next, and could not participate in after school activities because sleep would set in. Without it, she was much like she was as a baby—lethargic, disinterested, and disengaged. So when Dr. L. threatened to take the drug away, I knew that if she could stop using marijuana, she would.

Not only did she continue using marijuana, she was also smoking cigarettes.

As Maya approached her sixteenth birthday, her substance use continued. As bad as her behavior had been at times, it became even more bizarre. I'm not sure whether I believed my parenting had something to with her behavior or not, but I kept trying new strategies to get her to change.

*Journal entry: January 12, 2003*

*I've tried all I know how, so I'll try something I've always been opposed to: bribery. I'll give her an allowance of $3 per day if she's obedient. Her weekly account begins with $15, to be given each Sunday.*

## Credits:

| Task | Amount to be earned |
|---|---|
| Hang up clothes in bedroom | $.50 per school day = $2.50 |
| Load dishes daily | $1 per school day = $5 |
| Clean rabbit cage and carpet areas daily | $.50 per day = $3.50 |
| Give away three rabbits by Jan. 20 | Extra $15 |
| Wake up on your own daily | $1 per day = $5 |
| Mom nags (tells you to do something more than once) | $5 per incident |

Status checks were to be done at 10 p.m. each day, so everything had to be done by then! If she failed to do what is expected, debits would take effect.

### Debits:

| Task | Amount to be debited |
|---|---|
| Not getting out of bed by 6:10 a.m. on school days | $1 per school day |
| Forgetting to take meds | $1 per school day |
| Not cleaning rabbit cages/carpet | $.50 per day |
| Not hanging up clothes daily | $.50 per day |
| Forgetting to load the dishes | $1 per day |
| Missing curfew | 15 minutes late = $5<br>30 minutes late = $15<br>More than 30 minutes late = BIG TROUBLE |
| Smoking cigarettes/drinking or possessing alcohol or cigarettes | $10 |
| Smoking weed or anything else | MONEY CAN'T PAY FOR TROUBLE YOU'RE IN |
| Grades below B- | $10 per grade |
| Exceeding allowable peak minutes on cell phone | $10 per incident |

None of this worked, not only because of what was going on inside of Maya, but also because the system was too complicated to implement. I imagine it also failed because of what was going on inside of me, as over and over again, I was completely frustrated with her unwillingness to follow my rules. I began to question whether she *could* follow them, and became too exhausted to enforce the systems I had tried to put in place. In spite of it all, we kept going to therapy. We kept plugging along.

Because things seemed to be escalating, I felt it was time to get very specific and concrete about my concerns, so I created a list of issues to discuss with the therapist and faxed it to her.

*Journal entry: January 26, 2003, 8:36 p. m.*

### Concerns to Discuss with Therapist
- ***Premenstrual Dysphoric Disorder/Anxiety***
  - o  *Several-year history of problems during the premenstrual week.*
  - o  *Medication change? Primary care physician suggested switch from Zoloft to Prozac.*
- ***Restlessness/thrill seeking/euphoria***
  - o  *Need to get out of the house; puts herself in potentially dangerous situations because of this need to roam; associating with people she doesn't really know.*
- ***Smoking cigarettes and weed***
  - o  *Unhealthy and illegal!*
  - o  *Says she won't smoke weed anymore but wants to smoke cigs.*
  - o  *Says she enjoys the attention when she acts out.*
- ***Discomfort about ADHD and being in Special Ed***
  - o  *Says she wants to be "normal."*
  - o  *Hates being in LRC but it has served her very well.*
  - o  *She needs to see ADHD as a different learning style; perhaps needs to be in a school setting that fully understands*

*this learning difference w/o the stigma of Special Ed. Should I look for a special school?*

- *Unable to get out of bed each day*
  - *Can't wake up on her own—frustrating to get her to school each day!*
  - *Occasional insomnia.*
- *Inattention/time management/lacks "executive function"*
  - *Loses track of time; tends to be late; takes too long to complete a task; wanders.*
  - *Medication seems no longer effective; slow release Adderall seems not to be adequate.*

*Journal entry: January 28, 2003*

*Dear C.,*

*I have another concern—it's about Maya's memory. As I mentioned when we met last time, Maya had a meltdown at school last Friday and threatened not to come home at the end of the school day. She and I met with the tenth grade counselor and he and I were able to convince her to come home. She said that she really wanted to take piano lessons, so I agreed to provide her with lessons if she agreed to come home at the end of the day and to stop smoking weed.*

*I spent the weekend finding a piano teacher for her. When I finally did, Maya said that the piano lessons were my idea, not hers. She had no recollection of asking for them during the meeting with the counselor. My concern is that she forgets things a lot, even things she wants to do. She especially forgets things that she has said or discussions we've had. Her father had this problem too, except that he would say very mean things but could never remember having said them.*

*Maya also has problems retrieving words she wants to use and problems processing information. I think she gets frustrated when people talk to her for long periods of time, because she's having trouble processing all of the information.*

I never knew if her head injury may have had something to do with her memory problems. All I know is that the brain scans were all negative. Today, mental health professionals say that she should have received occupational therapy after the injury since she had problems doing math and with word retrieval. I couldn't help but wonder if this is just another example of African Americans not getting the quality of care that whites get. I know now that people with traumatic brain injuries also have problems with anger management and raging. I ask myself, which came first --- the problem with raging or the head injury? I think the answer is that the head injury only made matters worse. Not only did she probably suffer long-term brain damage, but emotionally, she was devastated at how the girls on the cheerleading team treated her. She never really got over it.

# X. Now I Know

*Journal entry: February 11, 2003*

*Today things started to turn really sour. The high school called twice to say that she was having a hard time holding it together, was "revved up" and angry, and was getting into verbal fights with other students. When I picked her up at 5:30 after Driver's Ed, she was sullen and wouldn't talk.*

*We went home to our little apartment, her going her way, me going mine. At about 7 p.m. I walked into her bedroom. She was sitting on her bed, about four feet from the TV, legs crossed Indian style. I was irritated by now—recalling the contacts from the school, wishing she would open up to me, and angry that she was watching TV when she was failing two classes. With obvious impatience in my voice, I told her to turn off the TV and get her homework done. I noticed she was rocking back and forth, sort of out of control, but in sync with the rap performers gyrating on the tube. She seemed to ignore me, which only made me angrier. I stomped over to her bed, grabbed the remote, and turned to shut the TV off.*

*In a split second, she became belligerent and flew into a rage. She tried to grab the remote from me. I pulled back, determined to be obeyed and to have the final say, and threw the remote across the room. She punched me in the face, pounding the nosepiece of my eyeglasses hard enough into my skin to draw blood. I couldn't believe what was happening. I was engaged in a fistfight with my daughter! I gained hold of my emotions long enough to realize that I had to restrain her to keep her from hitting me again. When she calmed down for a second, I got away from her and out of the room.*

*She started stuffing some items in her backpack, getting ready to leave the apartment. Somehow I had the presence of mind to realize that she was not herself, and that I couldn't allow her to leave. My greatest fear was that I would never find her again.*

*I remember going into the kitchen and noticing a knife on the counter, and for a fleeting moment, feeling an even greater fear that she might get hold of it. I grabbed it and pushed it into a drawer, and called 911. I had to do whatever I could to keep her from running into the night.*

My mind flew to my first cousin Paula, my Aunt Mary's daughter. An uncommonly beautiful girl, Paula was the same age as me. When she and I were growing up, I in Houston, she in Richmond, California, I liked her so much. She had a smart tongue about her and she smiled a lot. She liked the nightlife, liked the "bad boys," and didn't get along very well with her mother. When she was not much more than a teenager, she became a prostitute. Not long after, I heard she was addicted to heroin and in prison. I vaguely remember going to visit her in prison in California, when I was about fourteen. Finally, I heard she had AIDS. Every time I looked at Maya's life, I saw her going down Paula's path. I was determined to alter what seemed to be her destiny.

I also recalled why I had moved to downtown Birmingham. Maya often had the urge to walk outside, sometimes alone, sometimes with a destination in mind. So I figured that downtown Birmingham, an upscale community with quaint coffee shops, art galleries, and high-end clothing stores and restaurants would be a safe place to wander.

What I had not thought about was how different the police response might be.

Two young white policemen buzzed my doorbell at that moment and I buzzed them in. Maya seemed puzzled that someone was at the door, but she continued to pack. Soon they were knocking at the apartment door. They calmly and politely entered, asking what they could do to help. They looked like twenty-year-olds, and except for the pistols they were wearing on their hips, it was hard to take them seriously. They noticed the blood on my face, which up to that point I hadn't realized was there. One of them asked me to step in the back bedroom with him while the other officer stayed in the living room to talk with Maya.

Seated calmly on the edge of my bed, I explained that my daughter was certified emotionally impaired and that she seemed to be in some sort of crisis. I told him of our regular visits to a psychiatrist in the area and explained her medication regimen. The young officer said, "Well, I can see you aren't the one with the problem." I supposed that I was to be comforted by that, but then he asked his partner in the other room how things were going out there (with her).

The officers offered to charge Maya with domestic violence and I said no. They then observed that her moods were swinging from hysterical crying, to sucking her thumb and sitting on the floor, to begging them not to leave and clinging to their legs, to showing them her rabbits and artwork. They said she was "spiking" too much and one of the officers suggested she be taken to Beaumont Hospital for evaluation. Realizing she was out of control, Maya asked for more Zoloft to help her calm down. I gave her an additional 100 mg.

The policeman called for an ambulance, and soon I heard the scream of sirens. Somehow it didn't seem like an emergency to me because everything seemed to be moving in slow motion. I asked the police officers to please tell the ambulance driver to kill the sirens. All of the noise would agitate Maya more, and I didn't want people in our apartment building coming out of their units to stare. A few moments after the sirens were silenced, the paramedics appeared at my door.

They walked in calmly with very pleasant demeanors about them. They asked Maya how she was doing, and she thought it was just great that she had visitors. After taking her blood pressure and her pulse, they asked her to lie down on the stretcher. She did so gladly. This was an adventure to her, it seemed, but I was watching it all in shock. The paramedics strapped her in and wheeled her out of the apartment, down the hall, and to the elevator. I stood there motionless, not knowing what to do next.

As if reading my mind, one of the young policemen turned to me and said, "You're doing the right thing."

I asked, "Shall I follow in my car?"

He said, "Yes." So I grabbed my purse and keys.

Once I got into my car and pulled up behind the ambulance, I could see Maya inside, chatting away with the paramedics. I never knew if they sedated her. But she was showing no fear, no anger, no anxiety, just relief that she was getting help.

While following behind the ambulance, I picked up my cell phone and called my sister Pam in Houston. Speaking slowly, I told her what was happening. She told me to just pray, and everything would be all right. She had a tone in her voice that resonated of conviction and faith and her belief in God's power to make all of this all right. Her voice was calming and gave me the strength to keep my hands on the steering wheel and my foot on the accelerator. Without her encouragement and sensibility at that moment, I think I would have been too numb to move.

When we got to the emergency room, Maya was again swinging between sucking her thumb in the fetal position, sitting on my lap, and sleeping. She was hypersensitive to noise and smells—noticing and responding to everything—but at least she was calm. They released her from the hospital about midnight, but not before two unsettling conversations.

First, the psychiatrist on call took a thorough history but basically said there was nothing that could be done that night. They would evaluate her tomorrow if I admitted her, but they didn't have an adolescent psychiatry ward at that hospital. It seemed he was suggesting that hospitalization might be fruitless. "After all," he said, "She's calm now." So I told him I might as well take her home and let Dr. L. see her in his office the next day.

Then they sent in a social worker who began asking about my parenting style and how I set limits with Maya. I could see where this was going, but I'm sure she had no idea how that conversation would trigger me. How could I convince people that I had tried everything—therapy, autocracy, democracy, grounding, extra affection and attention, less affection and attention—and still it had brought us to this point? "This is not a parenting issue," I told the social worker, with fire in my voice. I thought to myself, I have a son who is a freshman at Duke. He was accepted into six top-notch universities, and got full rides to attend most of them. I've got a doctorate degree in maternal and child health, and an undergraduate degree in developmental psychology. "I'm a good parent!" I wanted to shout at her. Instead, I just grabbed my child by the hand and took her home.

*Journal entry: February 12, 2003*

*Dear Dr. L.,*

*Maya had to be taken to the ER at Beaumont Hospital last night. This happened after I received two calls from the school (different counselors) who reported she was having a hard time holding it together, was "revved up" and angry, and was getting into verbal altercations with other students, etc. I picked her up at 5:30 from driver's ed and she was sullen and didn't really want to talk.*

*At 7 p.m. I told her to turn off the TV and get her homework done, and she became very belligerent and flew into a rage. She punched me in the face hard enough to draw blood. I had to restrain her to keep her from hitting me again. She threatened to leave the house, packing up her stuff. I called 911 and the police came.*

*Maya has told me over the last two months that she feels out of control, is concerned she might harm herself or others, and I am seeing some personality indicators that are not really her. I thought it might be drug-induced but she insists she has not smoked weed since January 15 and isn't doing other drugs.*

*Please help us before she gets more violent. She has no friends. Her counselor told me yesterday that she is failing two courses because of missed assignments, and she has always been a conscientious (though disorganized) student. Please help us. She can't afford to miss more school so I'm taking her to school today. I'll give them a heads up about last night.*

I didn't tell Dr. L. right away why I left the ER that night. The psychiatrist on call there didn't ask any pertinent questions. He seemed totally unclear about what to do. He said that since she wasn't violent or out of control at that moment, there was really nothing they could do. When I told Dr. L. about this, he said that he couldn't hospitalize Maya either unless she was homicidal or suicidal. "Is she homicidal or suicidal?" he asked me. I had to say no because at that moment, she was calm. But only a few nights ago, I felt that she was going to hurt me. I had actually gone through all the drawers in the kitchen that night, hiding knives—just in case.

The next day at school was a day without incident. I picked her up at 2:40 p.m. as usual. She was pretty quiet all the way home, even a little sullen. I try to make light of things, as if the night before hadn't happened. I guess I didn't realize, although fifteen hours have passed since she punched me in the face, that my eyeglasses are sitting lop-sided on my nose. As we rode the elevator up to our apartment, she looked at me squarely and with sadness in her voice, said, "I'm sorry I bent your eyeglasses last night."

At that moment, hearing her sad remorse, I knew my baby had no control over what had happened the night before. I also realized that I, too, needed to lose my control act, my I've-got-it-all-together act. Not only was I not able to control her, deep inside I was completely out of control myself. Yet all the while, I was maintaining a perfect air of decorum, like a person in shock. No one knew that only the cruise control mechanism in my brain was keeping me moving forward.

Days later, things were still pretty shaky with her, but as divine providence would have it, this was the week we were required by law to update her IEP for special education. The IEP conference began that morning with the full multidisciplinary team in place. Everyone reported that Maya was a smart kid, and even a good kid, but something seemed not to be right. They asked me what Dr. L. was saying. I told them I had asked him to do more, but his response had been that he would need to hospitalize her to further diagnose her, and in order to hospitalize her, she had to be homicidal or suicidal. Why must we wait, I asked, until she's gone totally berserk to get the help she needs? Why must people cause death or harm to themselves or others before the mental health system will respond? How much sense does this make? Who is setting these crazy policies?

Next, they brought Maya into the room to get her input on how she thought school was going. They told her she would need to change her behavior, or she would be sent to the Children's Village.

The Village was a pre-adjudication center, a place where incorrigible kids were sent prior to being sent to jail. Hey! I had asked for more help, and this was their solution—to send my child away? I was shocked and dismayed. Unbelievable! I had done everything possible to get help for her, including begging her psychiatrist to consider a change in medication, but with no success. I had responded immediately to all requests from the school to discuss her behavior with me and to implement disciplinary actions. I had acted on every recommendation regarding counseling and seeking second opinions, yet their response is that the next step is to send her to a juvenile detention facility! This at the same time these so-called school "professionals" think her behavior is the result of an emotional disorder for which they have classified her as "certified emotionally impaired." Someone, *please* help me understand the logic of this.

At that moment I despised the head of the special education department, and every school around the country that had incarcerated black children out of expedience.

Suddenly, Maya said, "If you try to send me away, I'll fly off the roof of the school building." If what she said weren't so scary, it would have been funny. She said it with a matter-of-factness that made everyone know she meant it. This was not the "drama queen" talking. She meant it.

That was when Ms. D., the school social worker, decided to call Dr. L. Using carefully selected words, Ms. D. told him that Maya was suicidal. He agreed to admit her to a children's psychiatric hospital. Ms. D. agreed to go with me, and we immediately left school for the hospital. Maya was admitted on February 18, 2003, a month shy of her sixteenth birthday.

It was sad and painful to admit my little girl, but in a very real way, I was relieved. I would get the first good night's rest I could remember having in a very long time, and hopefully the doctors would find out what was wrong with her. The place looked like your typical hospital, but no one looked sick—not really. No IV's, bed gowns, or stethoscopes. All the kids looked normal, and so did their parents. A bit self-conscious as I sat in the waiting room, I hoped I looked normal too.

The intake social worker was a very young white woman who asked a lot of really insightful questions. I liked her. When I left there, Maya seemed content. In the throes of her quest for independence from her mother, I believed she relished not having to go home with me, with being able to spend an entire night away from me without breaking curfew. I knew I was in for a peaceful night's rest—the first one in maybe three years. The next day, Dr. L. came to see her.

By day three she was belligerent and angry that she had to be there. What started out as a great vacation away from Mom ended up being the place where people mistreated and traumatized her. The most important thing was that we finally knew what was wrong with her. Dr. L. diagnosed her with atypical bipolar disorder, along with ADHD.

She was hospitalized for a week, luckily while school was on spring break. Since she didn't miss any school, no one asked any questions when she returned a week later. Only the LRC teacher and the others on her multidisciplinary team knew. And now, I had to swallow my ego and tell the LRC teacher that she had been right—Maya indeed had bipolar disorder.

# XI. Is There Light at the End of this Tunnel?

When Maya came home from the hospital one week later, she was on Depakote, 1200 mg a day, and her trusted Adderall. She was a little sleepy and dull, but at least she wasn't out of control. I thought it was much too soon for her to be released from the hospital, but she was being released because of good behavior. Besides, the hospital said that the insurance company wouldn't pay unless she was still suicidal or homicidal. How strange is that, I asked myself. The powers that be would rather a sick person be out on the street risking themselves and others than pay for the care needed to keep her and others safe. There is something very wrong with our mental healthcare system.

I took her shopping to cheer her up. She had hated the psychiatric hospital. They had been very strict disciplinarians. She said they put her in a cold room all by herself with no shoes. She was totally traumatized by the whole experience, and wept as she talked about it over and over for several months after. This weeping was coming from a child who rarely cried or showed any vulnerability. I never felt sadder or guiltier for having allowed her to be sent there.

But when I was in my right mind, I remembered the kind words of the Birmingham police officer, as Maya was taken away to the hospital that night on a stretcher. "You are doing the right thing," he had said calmly and without apology.

Despite missing several school assignments in the weeks leading up to the hospitalization, Maya managed to actually bring her grades up during the months afterward. Perhaps it was the Depakote. But things got calmer, much calmer.

Now that she's been diagnosed as having bipolar disorder, I wonder if the Zoloft was actually the cause of so many of Maya's problems in middle school. About this time, I had been reading that when people with bipolar disorder are prescribed anti-depressants they can become manic. In retrospect, perhaps her early sexual activity, her constant need to talk on the phone (what the doctors call "push of speech"), her threats of suicide, and her angry outbursts were either caused or worsened by the Zoloft. With this kind of illness, though, and the lack of firm research in the treatment of children, it is very difficult to know.

But there is no benefit in looking back. I now believe we all did the best we could to help her, and no one could be accused of being neglectful in any way. I now see why identifying and treating a brain disorder is not easy, and of all the complicated mental illnesses out there, I can see why manic-depression is one of the most difficult to detect and treat.

Josh was coming home for spring break and was bringing his first serious girlfriend. It had been only a few weeks since Maya was released from the hospital. But her sixteenth birthday was approaching and with all she had gone through, she deserved a sweet sixteen. I'm not sure why, but my philosophy is that when things are chaotic, it's important to keep functioning in your typical routine. The structure of a routine keeps me focused on what's right and keeps me from becoming overwhelmed. This is why I always sent Maya back to school, even the day after an "episode." For me, routine and ritual had become salvation in the midst of chaos and confusion. For others, it might appear I was in denial or stuffing my feelings. And maybe they are right, but it's how I had learned to survive over the years—"Fake it 'til you make it." Or, "Smile, and before you know it, the world will be smiling with you ..."

So I began to plan a celebration. No one except my close girlfriends, my sister, my son, and her teachers knew about Maya's hospitalization. So I decided to behave as if it never happened. We were about to have a birthday party!

*Journal entry: March 15, 2003*

*Shhhhh! It's a Surprise!!!*

*Maya's Sweet Sixteen Bowling Party!*

*Saturday, March 15, 2003*

*4 – 6 p.m.*

*Hartfield Lanes and Lounge, 3490 W. 12 Mile Road*

*(between Coolidge and Greenfield in Berkley)*

*RSVP as soon as possible to Cassandra Joubert*

*(248) 732-8330*

The party went well and it was fun. Maya was completely surprised and felt like a princess. Josh had told her she was going bowling with his friends, and instead, we had the bowling alley filled with her high school classmates. Actually, they were the kids of African American parents I had met at the high school as chair of the African American Family Network (AAFN). I became involved with AAFN as way to connect with other people. By now I was feeling very isolated and cut off, having given up those connections to avoid being over stimulated. I ended up chairing the group, and it was great to mingle with other high school parents. It helped me to see the struggles that many of them were going through, not terribly unlike the struggles I was having with Maya, just less severe. We were great support for one another.

Even though the kids I invited weren't really Maya's friends, it didn't matter. The gathering was about fifteen kids, five or six parents, and another three or four of my closest girlfriends. There was cake, balloons, and gifts. It was perfect. No one would have known that just a couple of weeks before, this kid had been hospitalized and diagnosed with a serious brain disorder. The pictures from the party were like a still life—like life had stood still for just those few hours when we could pretend everything was all right.

*Journal entry: Choir Trip to Disney, March 30, 2003*

*It's only been fifteen days since Maya's birthday and only thirty-two days since she left the hospital, yet she's stable enough to make the choir trip to Disney! I am ecstatic that she'll get to have this experience, and the Lord knows I could use another break! It's not her first trip to Disney. She, one of her girlfriends, her brother, and I made the trip last year. But it's her first trip ever out of state without me, and that's a little late for a sixteen-year-old middle class kid. At least we know why she could never leave me before now—too much anxiety, too much fear of losing control, too much confusion about what was going on inside of her brain.*

I thought about going on the trip with her. I knew it might be hard for her, but I suppressed my anxious over-protectiveness and decided it was better to give her a chance to succeed at it alone. Besides, a year from now I want her to be able to take the several day-long Historically Black College Tour, so she needs to have some solo travel experience under her belt.

Her LRC teacher did not think this Disney trip was a good idea. Ms. G. e-mailed me the week before the trip sort of shocked that Maya's name was on the list. "I saw Maya's name on the trip list for the choir trip to Disney next week," she wrote. "Is this the plan?" I interpreted her comments to mean, "Are you sure she can handle this?" In my very-fed-up-with-the-school-system mindset, I'm thinking, does she think that after a year of anticipation and $1,000 in the travel agency's account that Maya wouldn't be going on this trip? Then again, that's not true. I've lost a boatload of money on plans that didn't work out for Maya. But, I've considered these losses to be a normal part of parenting, especially of a child with an emotional disorder. So even though I have paid for the trip in full (in fact, I overpaid, because I was too stressed during the last month to remember that I had already sent the final $250 payment), if I felt the trip would not be a healthy experience, I'd eat the monetary loss.

I wondered if the real issue here is that Ms. G. thinks Maya will be too much of a strain on the adult chaperones. I get the distinct impression over and over again that the "concern" expressed by the teachers in situations like this is not for the child's well-being, but for the comfort of the teachers.

Like the month before, when Maya made a joke in class. Several kids were entering geometry class just after lunch, still munching on the last of contents of their meals. Maya decided to pull out a snack—after all, the other kids were eating and the teacher didn't seem to mind. But, when Maya took the first bite, the teacher told her she wasn't allowed to eat in class. When she pointed out that others were eating also, she was told, "They are finishing up their lunch, but you are just starting."

In the concrete mind of a sixteen-year-old with ADHD (and even in the mind of a few intelligent adults), she could not fathom why it was okay for some kids to finish lunch in class while it was not okay for her to start. Eating in class equals eating in class, right? Wrong, according to the teacher. "It's because I'm black, isn't it?" Maya blurted out jokingly. After all, she really likes this geometry teacher. She believes he's a fair person, and her relationship with him up to that point was basically positive. Well, guess what? He threw her out of class.

It was Ms. G.'s job to resolve such conflicts and to be Maya's advocate. Maya explained what happened (and the geometry teacher corroborated Maya's recall of the events), but Ms. G. said Maya was out of line for disrupting the class, and for accusing the teacher of being racist. "After all," Ms. G. said, "teachers have lost their jobs over such accusations."

Wait a minute! Who's the customer here? Aren't the teachers there first and foremost to protect the students? What about dealing with Maya's perception that the policy of not eating in the classroom was being applied unfairly? Is anyone going to deal with that reality, or does that aspect get shoved under the rug so that the teacher's job is protected? In my mind, making the joke was a fairly mature way for a typically volatile ADHD kid to cope with what she perceived as unequal treatment.

Too often, the comfort and convenience of the teachers seems to be more of a driving force than the emotional health and well being of the students. Maya's IEP meeting just prior to her admission to the hospital is another example. Here is a child who has been struggling to survive in school for a year and a half. She had successfully managed to go six months without any problems or conflicts. She even received an award at school for an improved attitude and improvements in her schoolwork. For the last three months, however, she has had difficulties again: smoking on campus, suspensions for punching a kid who pushed her, bringing drug paraphernalia to school, being disrespectful to teachers. The school knows that during this same time, she is mourning her father's decision to remarry and move out of state, and that her brother just recently left to return to college. I'm not sure why bipolar and ADHD kids seem to suffer losses more deeply and to have fewer strategies for coping with them, but Maya had been that way since she was very, very young.

Anyway, she's been gone to Disney a full seventy-two hours now, and this morning came the first crisis. It may seem soon to some, but to have survived three days with no frantic call from her is miraculous! In fact, last night she called and talked over an hour. In some ways it was endearing, but in another sense, I can't help but wonder if it's a sign that she's trying to hold it all together?

This morning's tearful call gave me the answer. "Hi, Mom," she said.

"Hi sweetie!" I reply. "How's it going?"

She replies angrily, "Not good! They gave me my medicine this morning an hour late, and I told them I have to have it every day at the same time."

I say, "It's okay, sweetie. Nobody's perfect," using a line she often uses on me when I complain that her room is dirty or she's running late for school. "It's okay if you get the meds a little late. You'll be okay. It's just like on Saturday's when you sleep late. It's okay if you take it when you wake up."

She starts to cry. "But I want to come home."

I try to console her. "You'll be home in less than forty-eight hours," I say. "You can make it until then."

"What was the plan we made if I needed help?" she asks.

I say, "We decided you would go to Mr. Thomas, and you could call home whenever you needed to. Do you need me to talk with Mr. Thomas to let him know you need some emotional support?"

"I don't see Mr. Thomas right now, but Ms. Thomas is here," she says. She puts Ms. Thomas on the phone.

"Hi, Ms. Thomas," I say. "Maya is feeling a little weepy this morning, and just needs ten minutes of a pep talk and some emotional support. You know she struggles with sadness and she got her period on the first day of the trip, so that's not helping. Can you give her just ten minutes of a one-on-one? I think she'll be fine if she doesn't feel so alone."

Thank God for Ms. Thomas. I didn't feel embarrassed asking her to spend a little quality time with Maya. There are people I could never have asked to do that—those who don't understand special needs kids like Maya who appear so confident and yet are so fragile—those people would say I'm babying her, and would admonish her to act her age. That's one of the reasons I hesitate to leave her in the care of other people. They just really do not understand.

It's been three hours and the phone is silent. I think she made it through another valley moment.

*Journal entry: April 14, 2003*

*The Upper Room newsletter said: "Please take a moment to relax your mind, humble your heart and focus on God. Allow God, to be the only thing on your mind while you read this prayer."*

*Dear Lord,*

*I thank You for this day. I thank You for my being able to see and to hear this morning. I'm blessed because You are a forgiving God and an understanding God. You have done so much for me and You keep on blessing me. Forgive me this day for everything I have done, said, or thought that was not pleasing to you. I ask now for Your forgiveness.*

*Please keep me safe from all danger and harm. Help me to start this day with a new attitude and plenty of gratitude. Let me make the best of each and every day to clear my mind so that I can hear from You.*

*Please broaden my mind so that I can accept all things. Let me not whine and whimper about things over which I have no control. Let me continue to see sin through God's eyes and acknowledge it as evil. And when I sin, let me repent and confess with my mouth my wrongdoing, and receive the forgiveness of God.*

*And when this world closes in on me, let me remember Jesus' example—to slip away and find a quiet place to pray. It's the best response when I'm pushed beyond my limits. I know that when I can't pray, You listen to my heart. Continue to use me to do Your will.*

*Continue to bless me that I may be a blessing to others. Keep me strong that I may help the weak. Keep me uplifted that I may have words of encouragement for others. I pray for those who are lost and cannot find their way. I pray for those who are misjudged and misunderstood. I pray for those who do not know You intimately. I pray for those who will delete this without sharing it with others. I pray for those who do not believe. And I thank You that I believe.*

*I believe that God changes people and God changes things. I pray for all my sisters and brothers—for each and every family member in their households. I pray for peace, love, and joy in their homes; that they are out of debt; and that all their needs are met.*

*I pray that every eye that reads this knows there is no problem, circumstance or situation greater than God. Every battle is in Your hands for You to fight. I pray that these words are received into the hearts of everyone who sees them and everyone who confesses them willingly.*

*This is my prayer.*
*In Jesus' Name,*

*Amen.*

*Journal entry: April 28, 2003*

*I'm going crazy. I've got to get away. Shelley and I are going to St. Thomas. Thank God for Gail who agreed to stay nights with Maya while I'm away.*

I can get not one family member to keep her or stay with her, but Gail is stepping up to the plate. Gail, who is white, is a member of my church, and she teaches at a residential school for abused girls. Their behaviors are very similar to Maya's and according to Gail, these girls almost bleed negative energy.

Of course, all of my breaks are relative. There's no such thing as a complete break from an emotionally impaired child. Before I leave on any trip, making logistical arrangements for her is a management nightmare. Her every moment has to be structured and accounted for.

| Day of Week | To School With | Baseball Game?? | From School With | Spend Night Where? |
|---|---|---|---|---|
| Wednesday | *Sharnita* | *Yes – 4 p.m.* | *Sharnita; call her at (313) 388-3283* | *At home with Sharnita* |
| Thursday | *Sharnita* | *No* | *Sky will bring you home* | *At home with Sharnita* |
| Friday | *Sharnita* | *Yes – 4pm* | *Sky; call her at (248) 565-1598* | *Dondeena/ Sky* |
| Saturday | — | *Yes – Sky will take you to Groves* | — | *Dondeena/ Sky* |
| Sunday | — | — | — | *Dondeena/ Sky* |
| Monday | *Sky* | *No* | *Sky will bring you home* | *At home with Sharnita* |
| Tuesday | *Sharnita* | *No* | *Sky will bring you home* | *At home with Mom!!!* |

If she doesn't know exactly where she is supposed to be and when, she could have a meltdown. Over the years, "meltdown" had become the term for losing control, throwing a tantrum, or uncontrollably crying over not being able to either understand what's going on, have it her way, or, in other cases, not being able to cope. I've become a

"Maya-soldier"—doing things exactly the way she needs them done, in order to keep the peace and help her succeed. Relinquishing control over and over again.

I only received one frantic call from her while in St. Thomas. Maya wanted me to come home right away. Instead, I spoke with her for twenty minutes on my cell phone as I rode the ferry from St. Thomas to St. John. I needed to take care of me, and as long as it was okay with Gail, I was going to enjoy my vacation.

*Journal entry: May 27, 2003*

*Ms. G, I counted up the times Maya has missed LRC since February 1, and it totals eleven—seven missed due to therapy appointments, two due to hospitalization, one when she was out of town, and one when she was sick. That's eleven out of about twenty-eight (roughly 40 percent)! I didn't realize it had been so many. I see how this must have affected the timely completion of her assignments. Maybe this helps provide insight to her teachers also! Thanks again!*

*Journal entry: May, 2003*

*Hi Ms. G.,*

*I'd like to go ahead and pursue using the modified objectives for the classes in which Maya has a D- or E. As of today I think that includes Geometry, Biology, and English. I'm happy to come up and sign the papers either 7:30 tomorrow (then I'm off to Lansing and Flint) or anytime on Friday.*

*Also, her counselor said he'd speak with you about e-mailing Maya's teachers and asking for mercy. Thanks, Mr. W!*

*Meanwhile, thanks for speaking with Ms. L. about exchanging Environmental Sciences for Chemistry, and eliminating Algebra IIB until summer 2004. Please let me know the new schedule you come up with.*

*Also, I'll talk with Maya about the options we discussed today:*

*1) Having extended time on her finals (she'll be happy!);*

*2) Having daily LRC time next semester;*

*3) Continuing to use summer school to catch up on credits;*

*4) Visiting the Oakland Tech campus in the fall for possible enrollment in the Animal Sciences program there during second semester Junior year, and maybe completing the certificate program during her first year after leaving Groves.*

*I do plan for her to go on to a four-year college, but not until she's emotionally ready. As always, thanks to you, Brian and Kathy, for your hard work!!!!!!!!!!!!!!!!!*

# XII. Black Family Feuds

*Journal entry: May 9, 2003*

*Another trip home to Houston—starting out with excitement about the potential for feeling safe and secure—ending with the realization that this family might not always be able to provide me with that feeling. Whenever I come home, I feel I don't quite fit in with all the gossip, the criticizing, the yelling. And now the child I have with me is in danger of experiencing the same pain, the same rejection I sometimes felt as a child. How can I protect her; keep her from the daggers and dangers?*

I was born and raised in Houston, and three of my four siblings are still there. Both of my parents are deceased, and I often regret not staying in Houston so I could have spent more time with them before they passed away.

The visit started out well. I shared with the youngest of my three brothers Maya's recent hospitalization, the new medications, and the ongoing challenges. "I wish you had told me," he said.

"I would have prayed for you." I think to myself, "My hope is that you would pray for me always, not just during a crisis. And guess what? I need more than prayer. I need help!"

But instead I said, "It was all so traumatic that it was hard to talk about. Pam knew, but it was easier to keep it to myself, at least until I got through it. That's how I sometimes deal with things." Not surprisingly, he didn't really respond to this. First night at home—all things are much as predicted, so far.

The next day is my niece Shannon's graduation and it's a long day. Arise at 5 a.m.; be ready to leave at 6 a.m. to drive to College Station. How hard will I have to struggle to wake Maya up? How much will she resist? Will she willingly take her meds? How late will she be? I feel my anxiety increase by the moment. But somehow she is fairly perky when I wake her up and although her dress is a little "ripe" (her Dad's terminology for smelly), she puts it on, takes her meds, and looks pretty well put together, except for her hair. It's somewhat disheveled, but a little work with a scrunchy and it all comes together.

We make it to the graduation on time, manage to maneuver ourselves into some seats reserved for someone other than ourselves, take a load of family pictures, and then travel by car to the restaurant for the post-graduation luncheon. We get through all of this without significant incident. The restaurant menu offers a lot of options, perfect for picky eaters like Maya. She orders ravioli as the appetizer, lobster bisque, and salmon. We wait for the order to come. It's been six hours since breakfast and she's complaining of a headache and nausea. I see a slow boil starting to rise as she gets hungrier and thus, more irritable. We ask the waiter for some crackers and I suggest we take a walk through the winery outside to take the edge off.

Walking through the rows of miniature grapes helps, as she delights in their tiny-ness. My sister and her stepdaughter join us, and we enjoy the warmth of the sun and our discussion about the appropriateness of Texas weather for wine growing. Soon we are headed back inside the restaurant—calm, collected, and even pleasant.

We make it through the next three hours of another stop on campus, the ninety-minute ride home, and a long wait at the pharmacy for what was supposed to have been a quick stop to pick up photos from the one-hour service where we dropped them off twenty-four hours prior. By the time we get home, it's 7:30 p.m. and hunger is again surfacing. The planned menu is not suitable to my picky eater, so I agree to let her order a pizza. Out of nowhere, it seems, she explodes.

It's not the first time my daughter has yelled at me, or worse. But to my relatives, she has broken the cardinal black family rule of never, ever disrespecting your parents, and certainly not more than once! My brother lights into her with a yell, "Maya! You are out of line!"

Afraid that he will further escalate her, I say, "Cedric, I'll handle this." Wow! Now I've broken a cardinal rule of this black family—I've told my know-it-all attorney brother to butt out.

Sometimes it feels I am betraying my ancestors. How weak and ineffective must I be to let her talk to me this way? Children *do not* talk to their parents like this. Over the years I had been punished many times for disrespecting my parents. It absolutely was not something to be tolerated.

In parenting this bipolar child, I repeatedly found myself coming face up against everything I had been taught about how children ought to be handled. And the bigger battle was with me, constantly wondering if I was being a good parent.

If I chastise her or confront her, the situation with this child will only intensify. Is that what I want, another violent outburst to manage, just to prove that I'm in charge?

So I spoke with her calmly, perhaps appearing to my brothers to be just lying down and accepting her bad behavior. To them, I was just letting her get away with it. But to me, I was trying to manage the situation and not have it get out of control.

I recall a conversation with my sister-in-law right after Maya had gone home for her father's family reunion. She had said, "Maya was out of control at the reunion, acting out and doing whatever she wanted. Do you give her consequences?"

The question felt like a punch in the face. "Of course I give her consequences," I retort, "but she doesn't obey. Her bad behavior is not my fault. No matter what consequence I give her, she does exactly what she wants." Again, I sensed that Loy really didn't believe me.

When I was growing up, I never would have talked to my parents that way unless I wanted to lose my life. I can still see my mother's wild eyes right now, her open hand pulled back and ready to slap my face if I spoke just one more disrespectful word.

Years later, Maya's therapist would explain that bipolar children are harder to discipline. I think to myself, "No shit!" Meanwhile, I'm denied the *Good Housekeeping* Stamp of Approval for Good Parenting because my child is out of control and I can't handle her, can't make her stop yelling, can't make her stop smoking dope, can't make her keep her curfew, can't make her do anything she doesn't want to. The truth is, I couldn't get her to obey at age four, age ten, or age sixteen, and I still can't do it.

The psychology books tell me not to antagonize her, to be careful not to escalate intense situations. Yet, every time she yells or talks sassy to me, it triggers my black parent control button—the one that says, "If your child talks to you this way, they deserve to be knocked out. You are in charge, so act like it." Well, that advice, handed down from generation to generation, might work with some kids, but with a kid like Maya, it doesn't stop the bad behavior. It only increases it.

I would feel totally defeated and guilty, were it not for the advice of psychologists and psychiatrists. They tell me I'm doing the right thing, the best approach with bipolar children is to use logical consequences. If my daughter yells at me, I should tell her calmly that I don't like her yelling at me. If she misses her curfew, I should simply take the car away—no yelling, no angry words. Exercise discipline in a calm, matter-of-fact way, without yelling and punishing, just logical consequences.

All the studies I had read on parenting styles while I was in graduate school concluded that a parent's method of childrearing can have a profound effect on the child's self esteem and confidence, and the child's ability to exhibit appropriate responses to the conflicts and challenges that life inevitably brings. I knew the literature.

One researcher suggests three major categories of parenting: authoritarian, authoritative, and permissive.

The authoritarian parent believes in strict control and blind obedience and will seldom, if ever, offer the child an explanation of their rules. The child simply must obey. The authoritative parent, on the other hand, has just as much control, but faced with questioning from the child will try to explain the reasons behind certain rules and will take a child's personality and interests into account. Permissive parents basically neglect to discipline their child and let them get away with murder.

Although the conclusions vary, the children of the authoritative parent who exercises the more democratic form of control generally were better adjusted as adolescents. The authoritarian parent, however, tended to produce a less well-adjusted, insecure, and sometimes hostile and volatile child.

I ask myself, if the kind of parental inflexibility that black folk are used to can damage a healthy child, how much damage could being harsh inflict on a bipolar child? I had seen firsthand how Maya had been damaged by her father's approach to discipline. She always felt belittled and rejected by his harsh and controlling strategies. At one point he had even asked her if she was a whore. Pretty sweet words from Dad, right?

Although each of my siblings and other parents in my family believed I was neglecting to appropriately discipline my child and making a huge mistake, I know now that with her, I absolutely had to lose the control thing. I needed to be firm (authoritative) but not a dictator (authoritarian). What a novel idea!

It was my experience that black parents tend to try to control their children, not manage them. My parents always said that children are to be seen and not heard, and a child never raises a voice to a parent. Yet, my daughter was doing all those things and, to others, seeming to get away with it. Clearly, she knew better than to do the bad things she did because I had taught her better. But that didn't seem to matter. Nothing I tried seemed to matter.

Although it goes against decades of African-American teachings, I found myself wishing that black parents could understand that a bipolar child's disobedience or bad behavior is not a sign of disrespect, but a symptom of the illness. I could see firsthand that losing the need to control these children can mean giving them their dignity and helping them to succeed. I also knew that firm boundaries needed to be set for them as well. How could parents be taught to walk this tight rope?

# XIII. Aluta Continua: The Struggle Continues

After Maya was properly diagnosed and treated, I thought things would be much easier. But the more I read, the more I understood that bipolar illness is a chronic disorder and problems are bound to resurface.

I went around and around—thinking she was healthy when her behavior met my expectations, and thinking she was sick or relapsing whenever her behavior was out of control. Always though, the challenges just kept coming, non-stop, no relief, no reprieve. Even if things were better, I couldn't feel it. My life remained hard, challenged, and stressed. Even as I write these words, my child, now approaching adulthood, forgets her medication, gets into physical confrontations, associates with people I don't approve of, and because of unpredictable outbursts or failure to follow through on commitments, has difficulty holding a job and keeping friends.

Still, one thing I was always sure of was that she needed to graduate from high school with at least a 3.0 GPA. That may seem like a shallow, even inappropriate goal given her condition, but I knew my child was bright and I knew she could succeed in school. And getting into college was important to her future success.

Everything I knew told me to maintain high expectations, at least academically. I had lowered my expectations regarding her behavior. I began to accept her belligerence and verbal abuse as part of her illness. Her father's verbal abuse had led to our divorce. But I had no intention of divorcing my daughter and I knew that if she was to succeed in life, she had to finish high school and go on to college.

So I worked closely with her school to make sure that happened. I believe that this is the responsibility of any parent, but especially if the child suffers from a mental illness.

Her grades during the semester she was hospitalized weren't good, but she was managing to bring them up. I knew I had to help her perform well in school. As the semester went on, I was always fatigued. This whole thing was starting to take its toll on me. I was orchestrating her life day in and out—communicating with the school, shepherding her through therapy, managing her psychiatrist appointments and her medications—all the while trying to keep my male child focused on his college career and doing my own consulting work to pay the bills. I was paying his tuition all alone, taking his late night phone calls—my life was consumed with everything except anything for me. I wasn't dating, had no extra money or respite, and it was beginning to take its toll. I'll never really understand how I put it all on cruise control and kept on managing everything. My subscription to the *Upper Room* continued to provide daily e-prayers, which kept me lifted up and sane.

I wrote letters to Maya's therapist, and the teachers and deans at school as if I was her case manager. Besides, when I acted as case manager instead of just her mother, this fabricated role provided much needed emotional distance from what was happening to us both.

Between May and November 2003, things did calm down a bit. Maya attended summer school to make up for the one class she failed, and when fall came around, she began attending Oakland Technical School. OTECH offered a program in veterinary science, and Maya loved animals. Because the program was affiliated with her home high school, she attended OTECH in the morning and her home school in the afternoon. Finally, she started to look forward to going to school.

She was even placed at a vet clinic for a shadowing experience, similar to an internship.

Her counselors were surprised that I enrolled her in OTECH. They thought perhaps it was too soon, that she needed the structure of the regular high school day. But I could see that if something didn't change very soon, Maya would probably decide not to go to school at all.

She met a very nice young man at OTECH named Harvey, and next to Phillip back in Flint, Harvey was her best friend. They spent an awful lot of time together. He was a hemophiliac and in foster care. I met his foster parents and they seemed like wonderful people. I also thought it was healthy that they both had their disabilities, but could care for each other despite them.

That December, she and Harvey started to argue a lot. Maya also found herself involved with a group of boys who lived fast and loose. Before long, she and Harvey had broken up, and in February of the new year, while I was away on a business trip, she ran away from home. I had left her in the care of a woman who turned out to be totally ineffective in monitoring her. A desperate saga began with me trying to find her on the unsavory east side of Detroit. After three days of panic and sheer desperation on my part, she came home.

*Journal entry: February 2004*

*Dear Ms. D.,*

*Maya and I both saw Dr. L. this past Monday. Her last therapist was C.L., who is in the same practice with Dr. L. She saw C.L. for three or four months and discontinued with her last fall. Dr. L. has easy access to files that C.L. has on Maya.*

*You're right, we may have to seek other care but it's so frustrating to have to keep changing docs. You have a release on file to get info from the psychiatric hospital and since Dr. L. was the admitting doc, shouldn't that release be adequate to continue to communicate with him?*

*No, Maya isn't home yet but I did speak with her last night.*

Maya returned from the run-away, hair disheveled, eyes wild. She seemed to be racing inside her body, as if her internal motor was spinning out of control. I was reminded of my pregnancy with her. It always felt like she was somersaulting inside me. I thought to myself, "This must be what mania looks like."

Dr. L. agreed to see her that same day, but when I got there, he and I had a bit of a drag out. I thought his secretary had agreed over the phone that he would see Maya after lunch. Once we arrived there, he said if it was an emergency, I should have taken her to the emergency room rather than bring her to his office. He said I was possibly putting his other patients in danger by bringing her there. I told him that taking her to the ER would have been overkill since she was essentially calm now. I guess I convinced him because he agreed to see her later that day after hours, at 5:30 p.m.

But we didn't leave until I had also told him that his recommendation that she go to the ER was totally inappropriate care. He knew that Beaumont, the closest hospital, did not have an adolescent psychiatry unit. We had been there before with very poor results. Why would he suggest that we go there? She was no threat to anyone. She was completely calm and under control now, and sat quietly eating an ice cream cone while I blessed him out behind closed doors. I concluded that this provider was not truly concerned about this patient, and that other (more important) considerations were operating here. Yet, I wasn't entirely sure what they were. Nonetheless, we eventually left his office and returned at the designated time a few hours later.

Dr. L. started in again on her marijuana use. He again threatened to stop seeing her. At the time I didn't realize that he was concerned about liability. I later learned from Dr. Ann that bipolar kids who do drugs have a very high suicide rate, and many psychiatrists are really nervous about the possibility of a kid dying on their watch. I get that, but I don't get that threatening to throw the kid out of a medical practice or dumping her on a hospital emergency room is really that effective.

Although it had remained crystal clear to me that she cycled more with her period, when I spoke with him about that, Dr. L. just ignored it. As long as she wasn't threatening homicide or suicide, he was content to leave things the way they were. I wanted more. I believed she could be better, do better, be happier. She was either manic and running away from home, or despondent, hopeless, and confused.

I knew there had to be some consequences for her running away, even if she had been manic at the time. I went back to my disciplinary system of logical consequences. Again, I put the terms of our agreement in writing.

*Maya'a Violations – February 2004*
*1) Took car without permission;*
*2) Disobeyed grounding;*
*3) Drove outside of the designated area;*
*4) Stayed away from home without contacting me daily;*
*5) Did not fulfill responsibility for the pets.*

*Consequences*

*1) Grounded for two weeks: no social activities;*

*2) No cell phone for one month (March 23);*

*3) No car for two months (April 23);*

*4) Start seeing Darlene again.*

*To Get Driving Privileges and Cell Phone Returned*

*1) Get your driver's license from Secretary of State;*

*2) Attend school every day; no skipping;*

*3) Keep my rules regarding:*

> *a.   No guests when I'm not home;*
>
> *b.   Meet curfew;*
>
> *c.   Complete your chores;*
>
> *d.   Continue to take your meds.*

*If you demonstrate exceptionally good behavior, get the car back April 12.*

Amazingly, despite these consequences, she kept going to school and kept functioning. I felt victorious. I decided to find another psychiatrist, someone who would take the hormonal factors seriously, someone less punitive who would take a deeper interest in her.

Meanwhile, I finally found another psychotherapist who connected with Maya. Dr. Ann was seeing a number of kids from Maya's high school, and the school social worker had suggested her. Dr. Ann was wonderful. She was a warm and pleasant woman who used a psycho-educational approach. From the beginning she wanted Maya to understand her illness as well as she knew the cheers she recited at football games. What is bipolar illness, what's cycling? What are dopamine and serotonin? Her first several visits were purely educational. Maya, of course, resisted therapy nonetheless, but she liked Dr. Ann almost as much as her former therapist.

Therapy continued to be my idea though, with Maya going along only because I insisted. Even so, her attendance at therapy was sporadic. It became exhausting for me to always be the one making the appointments, ensuring that she got there, and paying the bills. Maya never talked very much, and a few times she actually went to therapy totally stoned and sat there like a zombie. Again, I was pissed.

I was doing all the freaking work here. I was trying to save her life, and she was getting high. Just writing about it makes me angry all over again. I was ready to give up on her. But the words of my colleague and friend Dr. Michael Carrera stood out in my mind: "The trick to raising good kids is to outlast them." Hearing his words, I affirmed to myself that I'm a good mother. I love her. I can't give up on her. So I sought drug treatment for her.

First we explored a residential program. The intake therapist interviewed Maya, and in her written intake summary expressed concern over her drug history, her sexual behavior, and her depression. She recommended Maya attend their year-round, school-based residential program—to the tune of $30,000.

That was out of the question. I was already in very deep financially with Josh at Duke. Plus, Maya's medications and doctor's visits were costing me hundreds of dollars each month. Even though I knew Maya was sick, I also felt that she had a will she was not exercising. I believed that if she wanted to improve, if she really wanted to stop hanging out with the druggies, if she wanted to make it in life, she could do it.

I found a non-residential program that basically used diversion tactics. Maya attended a few classes and seemed to enjoy them, but she lost interest as usual, and I lost the stamina to keep pushing her to go.

By now she was seventeen years old, and I felt that if she didn't want to correct her drug problem, there wasn't much I could do. I was exhausted. But I kept high expectations for her, especially academically.

Thanks to Dr. Ann, I found a new female psychiatrist who was also board certified in endocrinology. My prayer was that she would take seriously my observations that Maya's periods seriously affected her moods, and would do something about it. We drove thirty miles each month to her office, but it was every bit worth it. Dr. Stipic added Abilify to her daily dosage of Depakote and Adderall. She also put Maya on a three-month birth control method to minimize hormonal fluctuations that caused her moods to cycle. She gave me research articles to read and stayed on top of the latest developments in treatment. She introduced me to literature that discussed bipolar patterns in very young children, such as the work of Dr. Ira Glovinsky. Dr. Stipic was a God-send.

Maya improved, but because she continued to smoke marijuana, her moods continued to swing. When she was really high, she became hostile and violent. Dr. Stipic hung in there with her, never threatening her to stop treatment or toss her out of her practice. When Maya went into a manic period, Dr. Stipic stayed in contact with us by cell phone. Finally, we were getting good, solid health care. Now, if only Maya would stop the marijuana and comply with Dr. Stipic's guidance.

# XIV. All You Can Do Is ... Stand

*Journal entry: June 29, 2004, 2:07 p.m.*

*I don't know when my mind has been so idle, so unencumbered. It feels weird to not have anything to look forward to, or worry about. Maybe this is what people call relaxation, but I don't think my mind has known it in the past six years.*

*Maybe the problem is not how my mind is today, but rather how it has been in the past—filled with fear and anxiety about what Maya was doing, long lists of things to do to protect her and keep her safe, getting help for problems like substance abuse or disorganized thinking, worries about how to contain her chaotic behavior.*

*She left today for a visit with her Dad in Oklahoma. Two days ago, even yesterday, I was freaking out at the thought of whether she would remember to take her meds, whether her Dad would treat her unkindly, or leave her unattended. Will she be sad? Will she smoke marijuana? Will she go stark raving mad looking at the four walls? Will she and he not get along?*

I called ninety minutes after she left—thinking I might catch her changing planes in St. Louis. Her cell phone was turned off. So I anxiously checked the airline flight status online—both of her flights were on schedule. Not yet calm, I called her again when she was supposed to land in Tulsa. Now the cell phone was on, but no answer. She must have gotten there safely. And now I can breathe.

*Journal entry: September 2004*

*"He's too old for you," is what I heard over and over as I was growing up. Boys that were four, five, six years older wanted to take me out, and I wanted to be with them. Of course, I liked most boys regardless of their*

*assets or liabilities, so it's not that their seniority was especially alluring. But the rule was the rule: date boys your own age.*

*And now, as a parent of a seventeen-year-old, I was using those same words. Except, the logic behind the edict didn't seem to apply to my daughter. I mean, if any of my girlfriends knew I felt this way, they would surely accuse me of throwing my daughter to the wolves. But in my heart I felt that this older guy was the best thing that could happen to her.*

She's a very loving child, but she seemed starved for male attention. Her father was judgmental, harsh, and emotionally distant. Could this be the reason? Or was it because at too young of an age, the excess sexual energy of bipolar mania had overtaken her and resulted in being addicted to male attention? Perhaps it's a combination of the two. But it saddens me so deeply to see her depend on males for her sense of worth.

In October 2004, after several years of shutting myself off from all social activities in order to concentrate on my daughter, I met Michael. He was living in California at the time. In the beginning of our relationship, the one thing Michael and I had agreed on was that he would not interfere with my methods of rearing my daughter. He had no problem with that and fully respected Maya's place in my life. In fact, the first time he came to visit from California, I had wanted him to stay at the house with us. "You have to ask your daughter," he said. "She lives here, too." I asked Maya, and she said no!

She had been resistant to Michael at first because up until the time he and I started dating, Maya still slept in my bed. She needed the comfort. Lots of times she was suffering from anxiety and had nightmares. Things were going on inside her brain she couldn't control. I had talked with her therapists any number of times about how to get her out of my bed and sleeping comfortably in her own. Nothing I tried ever worked.

But once Michael arrived on the scene, she really had no choice. One day when Maya's psychiatrist asked how she felt about Michael, Maya said, "I really like him but I don't want him to replace me."

Seven months later, Michael moved to Michigan so we could be together. He was so kind and gentle towards Maya, and she quickly came to adore him. The difficult relationship between Maya and her father had robbed her of a supportive father-daughter relationship. For her to experience the love of a positive father figure like Michael was truly wonderful.

As for me, after years of emotional stress and trauma, I was beginning to open myself back up to the world, to defrost, as a trauma expert described it. Another colleague told me of scientific research that shows how the DNA of mothers who care for sick children structurally changes over time due to stress. Maybe this explains the sense of lost self that I feel. I look at myself in the mirror and wonder where I've gone. There are days when I don't seem to be in my body.

But there are also days that I feel a very strong sense of conviction. I find myself completely determined not to be hurt, used, abused, violated, or defeated by anyone—whether a lover, a neighbor, a boss, or a healthcare professional. I've come too far on this journey to fail now, and all that I have gone through shall not be in vain.

*Journal entry: November 14, 2004, 6:07 p.m.*

*Being agile. One of the most difficult parenting challenges I face is the constant need for agility. I find that when my daughter is stable, it is hard for me to treat her as a "normal" teenager, especially immediately after a period of instability, no matter how long or how short.*

*Tonight she left home about 5:30 p.m. to go visit a friend. She called home at 6:10 p.m. to ask if she could stay at the friend's for dinner. Because she had been so unstable just a couple of weeks before, my mind started to race about what was really going on—had she really been invited to dinner or was she meeting up with some character to smoke weed?*

*She was actually calling and asking for permission, not simply doing what she wanted without consulting me. Wasn't she? The endless doubts about being too lenient were matched with the second guesses about being too strict. Because my child is stable one day, or one minute or one hour, and then unstable the next, I swing like a pendulum between being the strict, no-nonsense parent and the reasonable balanced approach. To constantly swing like a pendulum is tiring and stressful, and I never seem to achieve just the right balance.*

I have no trouble remembering how high the stakes are, should I veer too much to the left or to the right. If I am overprotective when she's stable, she becomes angry and stops communicating with me. But open communication with a bipolar child is absolutely essential, according to all the experts. I've got to know as much as possible about what she is doing and feeling in order to keep her safe. As much as it hurts, I want to know when she is engaging in risky sex, smoking weed, or getting agitated. If I am aware of what she's doing, I can remind her of sexually transmitted diseases, the dangers of mixing her prescribed meds with illegal drugs, and the negative consequences of being belligerent with the wrong person.

When she was in middle school, I tried everything I could to keep her away from crowded, loosely supervised situations, such as football games or other sports activities, because it seemed these loud and over-stimulating events agitated her. She would find herself in an argument or fight because she had stuck her two cents in when she should have kept her mouth shut. The number of times the school called to report some altercation is too many to count.

In fact, the first time Maya recognized she was out of control and in need of help to rein herself back in was in middle school. I'll never forget it. Maya had gone to a teen dance at a local recreation center. According to her, the owners of the facility were badgering kids about not being able to re-enter once they left the building. Even though she was not directly involved, she became upset over what she thought was a silly or overly repressive policy and became argumentative with the owners. Not thirty minutes after I had dropped her off there, she called asking me to pick her up. When I asked why, she said, "I think I'm getting myself into trouble." That was music to my ears.

*Journal entry: March 9, 2005*

*As the alarm clock sounded in my bedroom, I rushed to silence it. Here I am writing in the computer room while Maya is asleep in my bed. The alarm starts with a slow ringing, and begins to accelerate, as I get closer to it. Maya raises her sleepy head and says, "Thank you, Mom," for coming in to turn off the alarm clock.*

*Such a simple thing—a thank you from my daughter in the wee hours of morning. So small, yet heart-warming to me after so many mornings of yelling, anger, and irritability. I reflect on the Bible scripture that has just come into my e-mail inbox from the Upper Room website:*

*Galatians 6:4-10*

*Do not be deceived; God is not mocked, for you reap whatever you sow. If you sow to your own flesh, you will reap corruption from the flesh; but if you sow to the Spirit, you will reap eternal life from the Spirit. So let us not grow weary in doing what is right, for we will reap at harvest time, if we do not give up. So then, whenever we have an opportunity, let us work for the good of all, and especially for those of the family of faith.*

In May 2005, Maya graduated from high school with a 3.0 GPA. She was completely pumped up and satisfied with herself. She also won several trophies for forensics in her senior year. Plus, she had been asked to stay at her part-time vet clinic job after graduation. She was doing really, really well and enrolled in community college that fall. Not soon after though, she forced my hand once more. I came home from work one day and found her and her boyfriend undressed in the basement. It was so very disrespectful of me, and I felt so used and abused to have given her the freedom and my trust, only to get this kind of disrespect in return.

I had also asked her over and over again to stop being a taxi service for her friends—driving them around town in my Jeep that I still owe more money on than it's worth, and that has a transmission that is about to go any minute. But no matter that I've told her this over and over again, she continued to run to the rescue of her so-called friends who use her and abuse her. I felt at the same time, that they were using and abusing me.

*Journal entry: March 12, 2006*

*The consequence for letting anyone in the house while I'm away is you must move out within thirty days, by April 12. (I don't really want her to move out. I want her to respect my rules, my space, my values, our home.)*

*Maya, you continue to violate every rule I set down, without any regard for me, or for yourself and the consequences. So, here are my expectations of you effective immediately.*

### *Stay Free of Drugs and Porn*
- *You will be drug tested every week.*
- *Take your meds on your own, morning and night.*

- *No pornography in this house.*
- *Make an appointment with Dr. Ann and see her every two weeks to work on our relationship.*

**Consequence: *If you test positive for drugs or use pornography here, I will park the car for as long as needed.***

### Cleaning Up

- *Clean up after yourself always, including kitchen and TV room.*
- *No food in your bedroom.*
- *Clean your stuff out of the box in the garage.*
- *Clean your room <u>every</u> weekend, including emptying all clothes baskets and returning them to the laundry room.*
- *Clean the downstairs bathroom <u>every</u> weekend.*
- *Clean Tiger's cage every Tuesday and Saturday.*
- *Feed Tiger and Sugar daily.*

**Consequence: Failure to clean means your cell phone will be turned off permanently.**

### Car Maintenance

- *Put the tire in the garage back into your car.*
- *Check oil and transmission fluid in your car <u>weekly</u> and refill as needed.*

*Since you continue to use your car as a taxi service: <u>All</u> gasoline and repairs are your responsibility from now on.*

### Money

*No more allowance. You will work for your spending money. I will pay for tuition, books, car payment, and car insurance just as I do for Josh, but no other money will be given (not for entertainment, hair needs, cosmetics, etc.).*

### *Respect for Me and My Personal Space*

*Because you continue to use my computer for pornography and then lie about it, you may no longer use my computer. Please remove your blank CD's and anything else you need out of my office.*

I go into my bedroom and light my candles to pray. I turn on Carlos Nakai and I talk with God. God says, "Take it slowly. Don't give her a long list of do's and don'ts. Just stop giving her weekly money. Fill the refrigerator with food, and tell her she can eat at home. Make her buy her own gas. As long as she agrees to go to school and work to pass her classes, continue to pay for her tuition, books, car payment, and insurance, and leave the rest to her. She can use the money from her job for anything else. That way you don't worry that she's using your money to drive her friends around and buy dope."

My problem is that I worry about how she's selling herself short, how she's letting the low-lifes use her, not just that my money goes to support them and their bad habits.

She left while I was in the bedroom. I'm not sure how long she has been gone. It's an hour or so later that I notice she has taken her week's supply of medication with her.

Is she running away again? Am I in for days of not knowing where she is, hours of worrying that I may never see her again? "Give her to God," Michael says. God, I sure hope your arms are empty tonight.

*Journal entry: March 12, 2006*

*Before I went to bed, I sent Maya a text message. "Where are you," I write.*

*"Far, far away," she replies. "It's obvious you don't want me around, so now you never have to worry about me anymore."*

*I tell her I don't want her to move, that I want her to respect my rules and me. "Do you love me?" I ask. She says "yes."*

*"I'll be sick with worry about you if you don't come home." She replies, "You should have thought about that before."*

*I say, "Parents make mistakes just like kids do." She says, "So now we're even."*

*I see her attempt to punish me, so I decide not to respond.*

*An hour or so later, she text messages me, "C u don't care."*

*I say, "What can I do?" She says, glibly, "Never mind. You're right." So I ask if she's coming home tonight. She says, "No."*

*About midnight, I finally fall asleep.*

Michael and I are planning to marry soon. In a way, I think of it as a reward for all the sacrifices I made to do right by my child.

This morning I remember some things I learned in my personal transformation class, about how we try to control and change other people and nothing changes with them. Yesterday, Joel Osteen's sermon on TV was on a similar topic: How parents stay too involved in their kids' lives once they become adults, and end up damaging their relationship.

I think back to a friend of mine who had also moved from Oklahoma to Detroit. She had a daughter a year or two younger than Maya. Her child exhibited some of the same symptoms I'd seen in Maya. I tried to tell her how important it was to find a way to get help for her daughter. Instead, she tried to control her rather than manage her. When things became difficult, as they always do with bipolar children, the child was sent to California to live with my friend's son. Nothing changed, the girl dropped out of school, and her mother didn't know where she was most of the time. It was very sad, and I wished I could do something to help.

Michael tells me how he used to criticize and judge his siblings for their unhealthy habits; then one day, he decided to just stop giving them money. He told them they owed him nothing and forgave all of the loans he'd made to them. But he stopped supporting their bad behavior.

I think that's the stand I will take with Maya: *"I will support all of your good habits. Rather than kicking you out, knowing you have no ability at this time to pay for your own place, this is what I'm committed to:*

- *I will pay your college tuition as long as you are serious about college.*
- *I will pay your car payment and insurance as long as you are in college.*
- *You can live and eat at home while you're in college, until age twenty-two.*
- *Cell phone is your responsibility. When you can pay for it up front, I'll turn it back on."*

No more threats. No more attempts to control her. I'm losing control, meaning that I am giving up the need to control—I'll just manage as well as I can. That's really all I can do.

Another year has passed. After two years of working at the veterinary clinic, and a year of taking classes at the community college, Maya has lost her job because she blew up at the office manager. The day before she lost her job, she punched a young woman at school because the woman called her the "N" word. The young woman filed charges. A warrant was issued for Maya's arrest, and campus police arrested her the next week for simple assault.

Here we go again on yet another roller coaster ride. Maya is older now, and I can't protect her from herself. Wherever she goes, there she is. Maybe the judicial system will be lenient with her. After all, it's her first offense. I've retained an attorney, but Michael says he doesn't understand why I am doing this. Maya's father sends a check to help with legal fees. He says we have to do what we can to keep her out of jail.

People say they don't let you have your meds when you're in jail. I worry about what this means for her future, her sanity, her life. She says she feels remorse for what she did. Yet, she still runs the streets at night, she won't settle down long enough to find another job, she's still hanging out with guys that hit her, and she's not doing especially well in her classes.

Both Michael and her father say that life will need to teach Maya some things that I simply can't. As a mother, I find it so hard to watch her fall. I have tried my best to save her. At the same time, I know that I can't live her life for her, nor can I completely protect her.

I just have to believe that what Joel Osteen said in his sermon this morning is true—that angel warriors have placed a hedge of protection around her—and around me.

When I was only ten years old, walking down the street in my segregated neighborhood in Houston, Texas, a station wagon, occupied with four white male teenagers, approached me. With no warning and unprovoked, one of the occupants threw Clorox bleach squarely into my eyes. I screamed and fell into the deep empty ditch next to the road. My young friends ran to get help, and a neighbor, Irene Hutchins, brought me into her home and flushed my eyes with clear water. She called my parents, and before long, they came to pick me up. They didn't take me to the hospital because in those days, the early 1960's, blacks could not count on getting good care from hospitals. In fact, some hospitals were still segregated. We had little recourse for fighting back, for getting the healthcare that is our constitutional right. We had no choice but to suffer through the hate crimes and the humiliation of racism day after day. The recent noose hangings and the Jena 6 trial are but one indication that we are still fighting that battle today.

Today, I'm compelled to take up a different, yet not unrelated fight — the fight for the rights of all families and children living with mental illness to get the care they need and deserve. It is my hope and solemn prayer that my child and all children in our nation, and indeed the world, find health and peace, and that those who read my story will be inspired to join me in that fight.

# SECTION TWO:

## A Clinical View

by Jan Hutchinson, MD, MPH

# I. Introduction

Lifelong messages can come in surprise packages. A medical school professor told our group of aspiring young doctors that being a good doctor did not mean knowing every single disease entity, but rather knowing what made up the range of normal. If we were to see something outside of that range, we would at least know there was a problem. It was okay to not know the exact nature of the problem. One could always get help. What was important was to identify that there was a problem.

Cassandra Joubert did that. As a devoted, loving mother, she knew that something was not quite right with her child.

---

*"Deep down I think I was already noticing that she was different in some way and was afraid to let myself feel my fear that the difference might not be good." —Cassandra Joubert*

---

She echoes the voice of every parent who has a child who is somehow different. There may be countless reasons for the behaviors and attitudes that seem unusual, difficult, and at times bizarre. The idea that a child has a mental disorder often brings the most fear, shame, and despair, particularly in the African American community, where the heritage of strength is expected to solve all problems. Over time, this courageous mother discovered that her daughter has an illness that is far more prevalent than previously thought.

The ancient Greeks and Romans are largely responsible for concepts of mood disorders. The Ebers papyrus of 1550 BC is the oldest known medical document. Among all of the diseases described, there is a discussion of severe despondency that is equivalent to what we now know as depression. Hippocrates (460 to circa 370 BC) advanced the idea that there are four humours (fluids) responsible for good bodily functions. The humor named "black bile" is now synonymous with melancholia. It is an aversion to food, despondency, sleeplessness, irritability, and restlessness. He suggested that the secretion of black bile from the spleen affects the brain, causing a darkening of mood. Soranus of Ephesus (98-138 AD), a Greek gynecologist, obstetrician, and pediatrician whose work influenced medicine for fifteen hundred years, was possibly the first to describe bipolar illness. He observed that a person may experience "madness" and sadness at the same time; that continued wakefulness can co-exist with alternating states of anger and joy. In 30 AD, Aulus Cornelius Celsus, a Roman encyclopedist, described "forms of madness that go no further than sadness." Aretaeus of Cappadocia (circa 150 AD) definitely made the connection. He commented, "It appears to me that melancholy is the commencement and a part of mania."

Furthermore, he described mania as, "Associated with joy, patient may laugh, play, dance night and day ... ideas are infinite ... believe they are experts in astronomy, philosophy, or poetry ... patients may have visual hallucinations, get noises and buzzing in ears, excitable, irritable, suspicious... bad dreams and sexual desires uncontrollable ... may change their mind readily... may kill his keeper and lay violent hands on himself."

In 1850, Jean-Pierre Falret described alternating mood symptoms as, "circular insanity," which was later described by Jules Baillaarger as, "folie a double forme." Other Greco-Roman doctors and scientists contributed to the understanding of the bipolar phenomenon over ancient centuries and cultures.

It was not until 1921 that Emil Kraepelin (1856-1926) recognized that severe mental illness could be differentiated by those who did not recover (dementia praecox or schizophrenia) and those who did recover (manic-depressive or what is now called bipolar illness). It was thought that these patients had a better prognosis because they were more likely to recover. Yet, patients with bipolar illness have a high incidence of co-occurring (multiple) disorders, suicide, and substance abuse rates, and few symptom-free periods.

# II. Clinical Characteristics

The term "bipolar" was coined in 1962. It is synonymous with the terms "bipolar illness" and "manic-depressive illness." Bipolar disorder (BPD) is an inheritable brain disorder, characterized by recurring shifts of mood, thought, energy, and behavior that impair the ability to function at home, work, school, and in the community. The Diagnostic and Statistical Manual (DSM-IV TR) has set guidelines for the diagnosis of various types of bipolar disorders: Bipolar I (BP-I), Bipolar II (BP-II), and Bipolar Disorder Not Otherwise Specified (BP-NOS).

BP-I involves recurring episodes of mania, abnormally "high" and/ or irritated mood, with or without depression. Unidentified, untreated mania often results in hospitalization, accidents, and/or incarceration. B-II is an alternating pattern between hypomania and depression. Hypomania literally means less mania. The intensity and duration of symptoms tend to be less and usually do not result in hospitalization.

Bipolar I persons are primarily manic and Bipolar II persons are predominantly depressed. It is hypothesized that BP-II is more common than BP-I. Bipolar II is more common among females than males.

BP-Not Otherwise Specified (BP-NOS) is defined as either the presence of elated mood, plus two associated symptoms, or irritable mood plus three associated symptoms, along with a change in the level of functioning. The symptoms must be present for at least four hours within a twenty-four-hour period for at least four cumulative days.

Manic symptoms may include over-inflated self-esteem, increased energy, decreased need for sleep, talking too much or too fast, distractibility, hypersexuality, daredevil acts, increased goal-directed activity, delusions, hallucinations, and a disregard of risky behaviors or activities that can have potentially painful consequences. The depressive symptoms may include a loss of interest in activities once enjoyed, a significant change in appetite or body weight, difficulty sleeping or oversleeping, physical agitation or slowing, loss of energy, feelings of worthlessness or inappropriate guilt, difficulty concentrating, and recurrent thoughts of death or suicide.

Definitions and descriptions of bipolar disorder in children and adolescents have been largely based on these definitions and symptoms in adults. A recent study of bipolar children and adolescents, ages seven to seventeen revealed that 57 percent had BP-I, 8 percent had BP-II, and 35 percent had BP-NOS. Thirty percent of the BP-NOS youth converted to either BP-I or BP-II during follow up. This suggests that the BP-NOS group has symptoms that are less precise than the symptoms of BP-I and BP-II. BP-NOS youth also had the longest time to remission. It took two and a half years on average as compared to nine months remission for the BP-I group and eleven months for the BP-II group. BP-NOS youth may also represent a precursor to adult BP-I and II. These findings are based primarily on the studies of Caucasians.

There is an ongoing, evolving understanding of what actually constitutes bipolar disorder in children. Are the core symptoms the same in children and adults? What defines mania/hypomania in youth? Is it valid to apply the DSM adult definition of bipolar when children are not usually able to overspend or to be hypersexual or to developmentally reflect adult type symptoms? Is it a completely different disorder in children, in adolescents, in adults? There is general agreement that mid- to late-adolescent-onset bipolar disorder is similar to adult bipolar disorder. However, the National Institute of Mental Health Research Roundtable on Prepubertal Bipolar Disorder (2001) determined that children can have either a "narrow" or "broad" phenotype (physical and constitutional manifestation). The narrow phenotype fits the BP I and II definitions. The children have multiple episodes with rapid cycling and their developmental stage reflects their symptoms.

Children with the broad phenotype are the majority. They have severe irritability, mood swings, severe temper outbursts, depression, anxiety, hyperactivity, poor concentration, and impulsivity. In other words, the symptoms are less definitive, may or may not represent early BP, and may be suggestive of other psychiatric disorders. One researcher has determined that a combination of mood disorder and behavioral problems may be a representative marker, or sign, of pediatric BP. There is a growing consensus that BP-NOS may be simply represented by brief bouts of mania that alternate with a depressive episode.

While much is in the process of discovery, there is agreement on several issues. Pediatric BPD is chronic with long episodes, episodes that include mixed and/or rapid cycling, irritability, comorbidity of ADHD, and anxiety disorders. The most common symptoms seem to be increased energy, distractibility and pressured speech. Elevated/euphoric mood, grandiosity, decreased need for sleep, racing thoughts and poor judgement are also common features.

Bipolar disorder in youth is also distinguished by the fact that they are more likely to "switch" and/or have manic and depressive symptoms at the same time. The presence of both moods simultaneously refers to a "mixed" state of bipolar illness. More than five to six shifts between moods define "rapid-cycling." Having a depressed mood with high energy and going from laughter to tears quickly typifies the disorder in children and adolescents. Fluctuations of mood may occur in the course of a day, several days or a few weeks. In one sample of bipolar children, 83 percent had mixed states. The symptoms tend to be continuous among youth but episodic in adults.

Maya had evidence of rapid cycling and mixed states. The argument that evolved into physical fighting between Maya and her mom was illustrative.

---

*"The officers offered to charge Maya with domestic violence and I said no. They then observed that her moods were swinging from hysterical crying, to sucking her thumb and sitting on the floor, to begging them not to leave (clinging to their legs), to showing them her rabbits and artwork." —Cassandra Joubert*

---

Diagnosis in children is complicated by a number of variables unique to that population. It is difficult for children to express themselves as fully as adults might because of language limitations. Development of vocabulary and self-expression comes with time, experience, and exposure. A child would be more inarticulate and lack knowledge of the proper words.

One must know well the course of normal human development because attributing bipolar-like symptoms to normal child and adolescent behaviors is easy. Children have frequent mood changes up to age ten. A child's cognitive, social, and biological development may determine behaviors and attitudes that, in isolation, look like bipolar symptoms. The behaviors and attitudes of bipolar children and youth are distinguished by their impaired ability to function in school, at a job, with peers, and with family. *The Child Bipolar Questionnaire* (*CBQ*) was developed to provide a rapid and economically feasible identification of childhood-onset bipolar disorder as defined by DSM-IV criteria and by alternate disease phenotypes.

Ms. Joubert, like many parents, initially attributed her daughter's behaviors to normal, although somewhat different, child development. Parents tend to think the behaviors are temporary, transient, or evidence of the kids-will-be-kids phenomenon. They quietly hope, wish, and pray that these behaviors will disappear.

# III. Etiology (Causes)

To date, there is no known single cause of bipolar illness. However, the National Institute of Mental Health has offered the theory that there is a problem in brain structure and function. Imaging studies have shown that the brains of people with bipolar disorder are different from those without bipolar disorder. Studies in children have suggested a variety of anatomical changes (e.g. small size of the amygdala and low hippocampal volume) and changes in brain matter (e.g. hyperintensity of the white matter of the brain). Changes in nervous system circuits may explain the impulsivity and irritability. The total range of chemical imbalances and structural differences has yet to be determined.

Because it tends to occur in families, researchers have focused on searching for specific genes. If one parent is bipolar, the risk that each child will be BP is 15-30 percent. If both parents have the disorder, the risk rises to 50-75 percent. The risk in siblings and fraternal twins is 15-25 percent. Identical twins have a 70 percent risk. Family studies have provided strong evidence of inheritability. The children of parents with bipolar disorder have been found to have a 2.7 times higher risk of any psychiatric disorder. They are also at four times higher risk of a mood disorder than are children of parents who do not have a psychiatric disorder.

Early onset of BPD is associated with a high family incidence of BPD. If both parents have a family history of BPD, their children show higher scores on scales of irritability, depression, rejection sensitivity, and lack of mood reactivity as compared to children who have one parent whose family history is positive for BPD.

Family history is extremely important. A familial history of mood disorders and/or substance abuse is highly suggestive. A recent study indicates that over 80 percent of children who have bipolar disorder are from families with a history of mood disorders and/or alcoholism on both sides of the family. There may be instances of a psychiatric hospitalization, of someone taking mind medicine, or of a nervous breakdown. Family members may talk about having to walk on eggshells around Cousin Joe, or how Aunt Betty has an unpredictable, volatile temper. There may be a family history of schizophrenia, gambling, or suicides. References to various members of Maya's family suggest that evaluations for a mood disorder might have been appropriate. Ms. Joubert described her cousin Paula as one who liked the night life, liked the bad boys, became a prostitute at age sixteen, was addicted to drugs, and served time in prison. She also describes her ex-husband as a high-energy, unpredictable person who alternated with an inertia mood.

Pediatric BPD has been associated with malformation of a specific chromosome. The bipolar genomic studies occurring across various United States sites are showing genetic linkages. One recent study of five thousand people from more than one thousand families showed a genetic linkage to regions on chromosomes. Some experts hypothesize that particular linkages may exist by racial grouping.

The "kindling" theory suggests that there are people who have a genetic predisposition to bipolar disorder. A series of stressful events may lower their threshold for mood changes. A variety of environmental events can "turn on" the already pre-wired genes. Several genes may be involved.

There is no blood test, genetics test, or brain scan that can make the definitive diagnosis. Psychiatric disorders that may be confused with bipolar disorder or occur along with it include depression, conduct disorder, oppositional-defiant disorder, attention deficit hyperactivity disorder (ADHD), panic disorder, generalized anxiety disorder, obsessive-compulsive disorder, and Tourette's Syndrome. Among adolescents, post-traumatic stress disorder, schizophrenia, and borderline personality traits may look like bipolar disorder.

Medical conditions that can mimic mood disorders include hormonal and metabolic disorders (Cushing's Disease, hyperparathyroidism, hyperthyroidism, hypothyroidism, hypoglycemia, and Wilson's Disease), infectious diseases (AIDS, hepatitis, influenza, mononucleosis, syphilis, viral pneumonias), neurological disorders (Kleine-Levin Syndrome, temporal lobe epilepsy), blood diseases (acute intermittent porpyria, iron-deficiency anemia), metal intoxications (manganese, mercury, thallium), nutritional disorders (pellagra, pernicious anemia), central nervous system cancers, and other diseases (chronic fatigue syndrome, Lyme disease, velo-cardio-facial syndrome). A complete work up that includes a physical and neurological exam, specific blood and urine tests, and other laboratory studies can rule out most of these disorders.

A link between childhood abuse and subsequent development of bipolar disorder has been theorized. A retrospective study of adult bipolar patients revealed that about half had histories of severe childhood trauma. Another study of bipolar adults with histories of child and adolescent physical and sexual abuse showed a history of earlier onset of bipolar illness, more drug and alcohol abuse, faster cycling frequencies, higher rates of suicide attempts, and a more severe course of illness than did bipolar persons with no abuse history.

Does trauma cause bipolar disorder or trigger an episode of bipolar disorder? There has been little investigation between the impact of other psychosocial stressors and the onset and duration of BPD. This relationship of negative life events, including low socioeconomic status, family conflicts, and poor family cohesion and organization, requires further investigation.

# IV. Prevalence Among People of Color

Bipolar disorder was initially thought to be a rare disease of older, upper-class Caucasians. But now we know that the prevalence is similar across racial and ethnic groups. One recent study suggests that Native Americans and African Americans have the highest incidence.

Clinicians misdiagnose and under-diagnose this problem, in general, and in people of color in particular. The clinical profile of people of color with bipolar disorder is largely unexplored. Several studies have shown that African Americans are more likely than Caucasians to receive a diagnosis of schizophrenia than of bipolar mood disorder.

Explanations vary. Some hypothesize that clinicians rely too much diagnostically on thought disorders that are characteristic of schizophrenia, ignoring and undervaluing symptoms of the affective, or emotional, disorders, and fail to recognize lack of awareness or judgment as a manifestation of affective illness. Perceptions remain that African Americans are not emotionally or cognitively able to experience signs and symptoms associated with depressive disorders like bipolar illness. One group of psychiatrists tested the hypothesis that clinicians are so distracted with symptoms of paranoia, delusions, and hallucinations, they fail to identify symptoms of depression in African American patients. Their findings did not support the hypothesis. However, they suggest that doctors may regard symptoms of psychosis as more important in diagnosing African Americans because these symptoms are more chronic and persistent than affective symptoms. A more challenging but difficult to prove theory is that there are simply racially based perceptions and beliefs among clinicians that affect diagnosis. Some regard schizophrenia as a more debilitating, violence-prone disorder of the lower class. After all, there are many doctors, lawyers, and other accomplished, respected members of society who are bipolar. They are high functioning when they adhere to treatment plans. People with schizophrenia, on the other hand, tend to have limited or partial responses to treatment. They are often unable to maintain a job, family, or home because of poor boundaries and limited insight into the importance of following treatment recommendations.

One must also consider the affect that cultural nuances in language and mannerisms and differences in communication between black patients and non-black doctors have on diagnosis.

Clinical characteristics and treatment history of African Americans and Caucasians do differ. African Americans in a bipolar registry have a greater number of inpatient hospitalizations and a higher suicide attempt rate. They were also more likely to report that a family member was schizophrenic. African Americans were less likely to report taking anti-manic medication but more likely to report taking anti-psychotics. People of color with bipolar disorder, in general, have higher rates of substance abuse and involuntary psychiatric commitment. One can only hypothesize that the inadequacies of diagnosis contribute to these outcomes.

# V. Prevalence Among Children

It is estimated that between five and six million American adults ages eighteen and older in any given year have bipolar disorder. The U.S. National Epidemiological Catchment Area (ECA) study measured the prevalence of various psychiatric disorders based on both clinical and community samples. Bipolar disorder has a lifetime prevalence of about 1.3 percent. The most recent data however, suggests that when one includes all levels of manic symptom severity, the prevalence rises to 5-8 percent.

Until recently, BPD was thought to be an illness of persons in their twenties and older. Awareness that this disorder occurs in children and adolescents has slowly evolved. Evidence for this is based on research findings, clinical experience, and family accounts. A NIMH-supported study has shown that the incidence among youth may be equal to that of adults. One percent of adolescents fourteen to eighteen years of age met criteria for BPD or cyclothymia, a similar but milder disorder. Six percent had episodes of chronic elevated, expansive, or irritable mood. The actual prevalence in children and adolescents is unknown. However, one conservative estimate is that 750,000 children and adolescents may have the disorder.

The rate of diagnosis is rising. Whether this is due to improved recognition by clinicians or to a real increase in the incidence of the disorder is unclear. Still, most children unfortunately remain undiagnosed.

Recent data suggest that children may experience BPD ten to twenty years earlier than their parents. The terms "cohort effect" (year of birth) and anticipation effect (generational) are used to describe the higher incidence of early onset BPD and the earlier age of onset in every generation following World War I. If a bipolar parent had illness onset at twenty-five years old and an offspring also developed bipolar illness, age of onset would be at fifteen. This represents an anticipation effect of about ten years. The National Depressive and Manic-Depressive Association study of 1993 reported that 59 percent of adult bipolar patients surveyed reported that symptoms first appeared during or before adolescence. Of this sample, 30 percent had very early onset (less than thirteen years old) and about 40 percent had early onset (thirteen to eighteen years).

The very early onset group had greater rates of anxiety and substance abuse disorders, more recurrences, shorter periods of stability, and a higher incidence of suicide attempts and violence. The Bipolar Collaborative Network (BCN) reports that 15 percent of the adults had a childhood onset. Some would argue that symptoms may be recognized as early as preschool (two to five years old) and latency (six to eleven years of age).

Early beginning symptoms of BPD typically show up ten to fifteen years before formal diagnosis and treatment. Although BPD has been recognized in all ethnic groups, research efforts are underway to bring better definition to prevalence and disease presentation among different racial/ethnic groups.

# VI. The Case of Maya

*"When Maya was born, I was fully prepared to stay at home with her to nurse for as long as possible. But I noticed right away that she was a very different baby from her brother. My son had enjoyed being rocked every night before bed, and nursing the first thing every morning. In contrast, Maya absolutely did not like being rocked. When it was time for bed each evening, rocking only made her fussier. I quickly learned that when she was ready for sleep, the most effective way to calm her was to swaddle her in a blanket and simply lay her in her crib—no rocking, no music ... just quiet."* —*Cassandra Joubert*

Some clinicians and caretakers in retrospect believe that signs and symptoms of BPD can occur during the toddler and preschool stage. Temperamental and behavioral traits of irritability, inflexibility, and opposition are common. Excessively loud, excessively long temper tantrums (called rages or affective storms) are common during the early childhood of BPD youth. Maya's temper tantrums lasted five to ten minutes when confronted with a no. Tantrums in BPD children can last for hours. Those associated with whining and crying tend to last longer. Children and adolescents are more likely than adults to be irritable and to have destructive, negative outbursts. For example, while in elementary school, Maya punched a classmate. Behaviors can be reckless and dangerous.

Admittedly, children can demonstrate impulsive and aggressive behaviors for a variety of reasons. Consistently unpredictable triggers should alert parents and guardians to a possible diagnosis of BPD. These children also have a questionable higher rate of physical injury than do other children.

Ms. Joubert noted that Maya was an explosive, volatile child at an early age. A first-grade teacher noted that Maya tended to overreact to natural, normal events, e.g. someone stepping on her toe. Sensitivity to noise and to other sensory stimuli was evident when Maya was a newborn. Quiet and swaddling seemed to comfort her to sleep. The activity, noise, and stimulation of the Day School seemed to frustrate her. The clamor of dishes and pots was irritating. Transitions were difficult, irritating and painful to be precise. In or out of the tub, getting dressed or undressing provoked her to tears. Maya's response to her first spanking at four years old was emotionless; according to Ms. Joubert, "The stubbornness was striking." These children often have a willfulness about them that is both disturbing and frustrating. They relentlessly insist on having things their way. Verbal and/or physical attacks on parents may occur. Disagreements are intense. Flexibility and cooperation with the most simple request or expectation can be elusive.

Ms. Joubert did not know that inconsolable tantrums, noise sensitivity, oppositional defiance, and difficult transitions are early clues that a bipolar illness may be present.

In first grade, Maya was noted to be extremely clingy to her mother and had a hard time separating from her. These are two of the major symptoms of separation anxiety. Separation anxiety and temper tantrums can occur during either a manic or depressive phase.

The first symptom of bipolar illness in children and adolescents is depression in one third of cases. Chronic irritability, sadness, and lack of desire to engage in pleasurable activities may be present. Depression among youth may be manifested as headaches, stomach aches, fatigue, muscle aches, poor or declining grades, efforts to run away, easy and frequent crying, impaired communication and relationships, sensitivity to rejection or failure, and alcohol or substance abuse. While depression tends to be the initial presenting symptom to the clinician, manic or hypomanic symptoms may be more sensational and provocative. Depressive episodes tend to last far longer than manic or hypomanic episodes, start at earlier ages in the life cycle, and last for longer periods than mania.

The dilemma for the clinician lies in which type of depression is represented. Is this a dysthymic disorder, a mild depression of two years duration with fewer, less intense symptoms? Is it a major depressive disorder, a more serious depression of at least two weeks duration in which there is severe hopelessness, sadness, and feelings of worthlessness, occasionally occurring in association with psychotic symptoms? Or is it the depression of bipolar illness in which episodes of depression may occur, but in which there are manic or hypomanic symptoms? Distinguishing one type from another may occur over weeks, months, or years depending on the evolution of symptoms.

---

*"If you try to send me away, I'll fly off the roof of the school building,"*
*Maya told them. If what she said weren't so scary, it would have been*
*funny. She said it with a matter-of-factness that made everyone know she*
*meant it. This was no drama queen talking." —Cassandra Joubert*

---

Bipolar persons have a higher incidence of suicide than the general population. Bipolar children may express suicidal ideation, talk of wanting to die. The plan in young preschool or latency age children is to run into traffic or to jump out of a moving car.

Maya first expressed suicidal ideation and a suicide attempt as an eighth grader. Upset and sad that her grandparents had not attended Grandparents Day, she decided to hold her breath because she didn't want to live anymore. The school mistook this suicide effort as an asthma attack. In another incident, she threatened to jump off the roof of the school building.

In one study, children aged seven to seventeen who attempted suicide were more likely to have a lifetime history of comorbid substance use disorder, panic disorder, non-suicidal self-injurious behavior, family history of suicide attempt, history of hospitalization, and history of physical and/or sexual abuse. Suicidal ideation more likely occurs during a depressive or mixed episode. Youth who do present with depression in the initial phase rather than mania or hypomania are at increased risk for suicidal behavior, repeated suicide attempts, and completed suicide.

# VII. ADHD versus BPD

---

*"First Grade - And after all, Maya's diagnosis in first grade of borderline, rather than full ADHD was because she didn't fully meet the criteria for ADHD at that time. When the doctor prescribed Ritalin, it was done with the attitude of, "Let's try this to see if it helps. If it helps, then she probably has ADHD. If it doesn't help, she must not have it."*

*Seventh Grade* - *Maya seemed angry so much of the time, so I re-enrolled her in therapy, this time an anger management class. Before the social worker would accept her, she conducted a psychological evaluation and concluded that Maya had obsessive-compulsive disorder (OCD) and oppositional defiant disorder (ODD).*

*Eighth grade* - *Her teachers said she was brilliant, but her grades were only mediocre. I decided to get another psychological evaluation and educational assessment, and landed upon the best psychologist we had ever had. Dr. Max Taylor diagnosed her with ADHD and impulse control disorder, and said he saw little evidence of OCD and ODD. He also said she had an IQ in the superior range."* —*Cassandra Joubert*

---

Diagnosis in children is further complicated by the similarities between bipolar disorder and attention deficit hyperactivity disorder (ADHD). The symptoms of distractibility, impulsivity, and hyperactivity may exist in either disorder, represent an early indication of BPD, or co-exist. Substance abuse is seen in both disorders. Still, there are distinct differences between BPD and ADHD.

The anger and range of a temper tantrum in the bipolar child may be more severe in intensity and last for hours. Bipolar children react strongly to being told no and to not having things as they want them. Manic expressions of physical and emotional energy result in destructiveness that may even be sadistic. Tantrums in the child with ADHD usually last less than twenty minutes and are less intense. Sensory and emotional over-stimulation is the source of their tantrums. Moods of bipolar children are more likely to show depression and irritability. These children are also more likely to provoke others or challenge authority, while the misdeeds of children with ADHD are more likely unintentional and are secondary to inattentiveness.

Despite the elusiveness of sleep, persons with bipolar illness are energetic during daily activities, while persons with ADHD have more normative sleep patterns. The absence of sleep leaves them fatigued and inactive.

Bipolar youth are risk-seeking, while ADHD children may accidentally or unintentionally involve themselves in behaviors that are dangerous. Creativity and artistic flair are frequently found in bipolar youth, but not in ADHD youth. Therefore, bipolar youth may enjoy more popularity than ADHD youth, who are often seen as irritating and intrusive. Perceptions of reality (delusions and hallucinations) may be distorted in bipolar children, but are usually intact in ADHD children.

An unusual and strong interest in sex is a common finding in bipolar youth, but not in ADHD youth. Hypersexuality occurs in 24 percent prior to puberty and in 70 percent after puberty. It occurs in only 8 percent of ADHD children.

The person with ADHD is not engaging in excessive goal-directed activities and hardly completes any task before starting the next one. Suicidal plans or intent occur in 27 percent of bipolar youth, versus a much lower percent of those with ADHD. It has been suggested that bipolar children have higher IQs than ADHD children. And finally, responses to medications vary greatly depending on whether the child is bipolar or ADHD. The symptoms of bipolar illness do not respond to treatment with stimulants, nor do the symptoms of ADHD respond to mood stabilizers.

Maya is an example of many aspects of the convergence and divergence of symptoms between ADHD and BPD. The kindergarten teacher observed that five-year-old Maya was an explosive, emotionally volatile child. This led to a psychological examination that determined that she had five of the required six symptoms of ADHD. A tentative diagnosis of borderline ADHD was made although Maya did not show signs of physical hyperactivity nor did she seem to have symptoms in more than one setting. A diagnosis of ADHD requires that impairments to function occur in more than one setting (e.g. school, home, and/or work.)

Ritalin did seem to have the positive effect associated with a diagnosis of ADHD. Maya seemed more alert, expressive, engaged, and mentally present. Grades improved. Stimulant medications like Ritalin tend to improve focus and decrease impulsivity and hyperactivity in most children and adults.

ADHD is the most commonly diagnosed mental disorder in children, usually presenting before seven years old. However, antenna should have been rising because although the hyperactive-impulsive type common in males is probably more prevalent in females than recognized and female children are more likely to present with the inattentive type of ADHD. ADHD children do not usually have volatile temperaments. As previously noted, ADHD and BPD often co-exist. Or, early signs of BPD may be mistaken for signs of ADHD. In addition, nearly all childhood mental disorders present with impulsivity and aggression. Good medical practice requires careful, thoughtful monitoring of the course and development of symptoms.

Maya had many of the classic signs of bipolar disorder present in both children and adults. Ms. Joubert bravely discusses the hypersexuality, an issue about which most parents feel disquieted and embarrassed.

*"Then one day when she had just completed the sixth grade, I got a call from a neighbor that she had seen two boys enter my home after school that day. When I arrived home and asked Maya about it, she casually admitted that the two boys had been there, and that she had sex with both of them, each while the other watched."* —**Cassandra Joubert**

A dictionary definition of "hypersexual" is: unusually or excessively interested in or concerned with sexual activity. This interest may present as excessive or unconcealed masturbation, sexualized language, and/or a fascination with and touching or rubbing of private parts of other people. Some children hug or kiss in a sensual way. In older children, repetitive calls to phone sex lines and repeated trips to the bathroom to self-stimulate should raise suspicion. Older children and teens will also engage in multiple, indiscriminate sexual acts. The sexual contacts are usually unprotected, and therefore sometimes result in sexually transmitted diseases.

Rumors of sexual indiscretion were rampant when Maya was an eleven-year-old sixth grader. Sexual activity became definitely voluntary at age twelve when Maya had sex with two neighbor boys. While mom was alarmed, the daughter was not.

Hypersexuality in a child should suggest one of two possibilities. The first consideration is whether the child has been sexually abused. Females abused early in life often will engage in multiple sexual liaisons with any male, including those who they barely know or don't know at all. The behavior has a compulsive quality and the child does not recognize it as dangerous, inappropriate, or unusual. It should be noted, however, that sexual abuse may also trigger hypersexual behavior in a bipolar-disposed child.

If one can rule out sexual abuse as the source of the symptom, the second consideration should be whether the child is bipolar. Hypersexuality related to bipolar illness suggests that the youth is in either a manic or hypomanic phase. A recent study revealed that 43 percent of a group of manic bipolar children were also hypersexual. It has been hypothesized that this sexuality is an expression of the extreme impulsivity characteristic of the illness. These kids transgress boundaries in general and especially sexual boundaries.

The science of medicine has not yet explained this excess, but the important point here is that people should not judge it as promiscuity. It is critical that the doctor, the parents, the child, and all others understand the behavior as a symptom of an illness, not a willful bad behavior that requires punishment. Pejorative comments delay diagnosis, impede treatment, and blame the victim.

Hypersexuality is but one presentation of mania. Other symptoms can include overspending (e.g. excessive credit card charges), pressured speech and fast talking, grandiose thinking, daredevil acts and behavioral disruptions, a decreased need for sleep, and an excessively elated or expansive mood. Over the course of a child's growth and development, there can be many faces of mania. One has to wonder even about gestational presentation. Ms. Joubert said that during her pregnancy, Maya always felt like she was somersaulting inside me. This thought resurfaces as Ms. Joubert recalls Maya's appearance after a runaway episode at age thirteen. "She seemed to be racing inside her body, as if there was an internal motor out of control ... hair was disheveled ... eyes were wild ... this must be what mania looks like," said Joubert.

The compulsive calling of friends, one after the other, while in middle school suggests the driven, intense, quality of mania. In seventh grade, signs of grandiosity surfaced when Maya exclaimed that she preferred to attend a certain school because she wouldn't want to disappoint them by going somewhere else. Sometimes grandiosity takes the form of a child complaint that the teacher doesn't know how to teach and that they know more than the teacher. Other children will say that they have been accepted at a school of academic excellence, when in reality they are failing most subjects.

People with bipolar illness are extra sensitive to many stimuli, giving them a chronically irritable mood. A look, a comment, a gesture that is innocent and benign becomes the source of loud, rancorous displeasure. Bipolar children are likely to misinterpret facial expressions and nonverbal cues of other children, reading sadness as happiness and fear as anger. This may in part explain the poor social skills, lack of friends, and teasing by other children found in at least 50 percent of bipolar children.

Ms. Joubert repeatedly observes that Maya seemed isolated, with few friends as she moved through the elementary school years. In Maya's case, the cruelty and lack of understanding from other classmates resulted in cruel and devious outcomes for Maya. She became the scapegoat for all negative, destructive behaviors, e.g. accusations that she had developed a hit list of classmates to harm.

Bipolar children and adolescents often have several incidents of detention, suspension, and expulsion from school. Society tends to regard these youth as bad kids. As teens and young adults, they may be regarded as simply antisocial. Breaking rules and challenging authority may have many causes, the irritability and impulsivity of BPD may be among them, and one should consider and evaluate such youth for the disorder.

Maya punched a classmate in the stomach on one occasion and was expelled after making a threatening gesture with a knife. A frequent or chronic inability to exercise self-control to the extent that it impairs functionality deserves investigation. An estimated 10 percent of incarcerated adults have bipolar disorder.

# VIII. Comorbidity

Over 60 percent of bipolar patients develop a substance abuse disorder over the lifetime course of the illness. The substance abuse can occur before or after the appearance of affective or manic symptoms. Alcohol and cocaine are the most popular agents.

In Maya's case, alcohol and marijuana use occurred early in the teen years. Finding drug paraphernalia and drugs was a recurring frustration for Ms. Joubert. Bipolar patients who have a substance abuse disorder have a higher incidence of depression, poor treatment compliance, and a generally worsened course. Some researchers speculate that drug use by bipolar persons is an attempt to self-treat. However, the substance abuse should then rise and fall with the depression episodes. The data to date does not support this hypothesis. At least one study has shown that there is no correlation between affective symptoms and substance abuse. Others feel that the high incidence of drug abuse is related to the impulsivity and poor judgment that is a part of the disorder. Impulsivity, a characteristic of mania, is common in both substance abusers and persons with bipolar illness.

Drinking behavior does not seem to change in response to depressive or manic episodes. Even if a bipolar person is feeling depressed or has a stable mood, they may continue to be impulsive. It should be pointed out that bipolar patients often will skip their medications, but are often eager and chronic abusers of street drugs. One hypothesis that remains to be tested is that street drugs maintain and stimulate the mania or hypomania while treatment medications take away or reduce the high that some of these patients say they enjoy and don't want to give up.

Anxiety also often accompanies bipolar illness. It has already been noted that Maya had signs of separation anxiety as a very young child. In third grade, other signs of anxiety emerged: her distaste for crowds, which left her quiet, anxious, and clingy. Ms. Joubert had to pick her up from school as soon as class ended; otherwise, Maya became fearful and anxious.

As a little girl, Maya would awaken and go to her parents' room. This is a common childhood behavior of the night. But later, as an older child, Maya was still coming into her parents' bed. Certainly explanations can vary. Perhaps she was afraid, anxious, lonely, or depressed. Symptoms can represent a variety of illnesses and problems, so conducting careful investigations is important.

Throughout the narrative, Maya's moods worsen up to one week prior to the monthly onset of menses. "It seemed that the week before Maya's period was always the most challenging time for her—anger and sadness and irritability, conflicts at school and at home—a pattern," explained Joubert. Female reproductive hormones seem to impact the course of bipolar disorder in females. Hormonal fluctuations appear to be associated with increased risk of mood swings in women with bipolar disorder.

New information from the Systematic Treatment Enhancement Program for Bipolar Disorder (STEP-BD) suggests that women may have a different presentation of the illness than men. Female adults are more likely to have Bipolar II, more comorbid thyroid disease, higher rates of bulimia, and posttraumatic stress disorder. STEP-BD findings also suggest that women with bipolar disorder were significantly more likely to have early onset menstrual dysfunction than women with unipolar depression or healthy women.

# IX. Early Diagnosis

Early recognition and diagnosis is one of the biggest frustrations for parents of bipolar children. Certainly the challenges of moving, divorce, marital strife, disagreeable and unsupportive family and friends, school challenges, and other insults to daily living can provoke personality changes and maladaptive responses. The idea that a mental illness is as possible, real, and difficult to manage as a physical illness is an unacceptable thought for most. People of color seem to be even less receptive.

For African American parents, the frustration is complicated by the burden of living in an environment that is historically unfriendly to people of color. Survival requires considerable emotional energy to defend and protect from any unfriendly fire—whether real or misperceived.

The seeds of suspicion and distrust that prevent and delay mental disorder diagnoses and treatment among African Americans were planted during slavery.

Prominent physician Dr. Benjamin Rush, known as the father of American psychiatry and a leading mental health reformer and co-founder of the first anti-slavery society in America, referred to the condition of slaves as "negritude," a mild form of leprosy.

Louisiana physician and general practitioner Dr. Sam Cartwright identified two mental disorders peculiar to slaves. He identified the practice of running away from slavery as "Drapetomania." Preventing this behavior of sulkiness and dissatisfaction required the therapeutic early intervention of keeping the Negro in a submissive state and treating them like children with care and attention. He identified still another condition as "Dysaethesia Aethipica." This referred to dullness of the mind or "rascality." This was explained to be different from other mental diseases because there were physical signs and lesions of whipping. These, of course, were inflicted as the decided cure for rascality.

The Superintendent of the Georgia Lunatic Asylum espoused the belief that freedom for slaves resulted in insanity and that slavery provided hygienic, structured protection. Psychiatric and physical medicine embraced the notion that a mentally healthy slave was content with his condition; protest reflected derangement.

Slaves were perceived to have a primitive psychological organization that was uniquely fit for slavery. Mental health professionals like psychologist G. Stanley Hall supported these ideas. He was one of the founders of the American Psychological Association and the American Journal of Psychology. He believed that, "Africans, Indians, and Chinese are adolescent races in a stage of incomplete growth."

In more modern times, the Tuskegee Syphilis experiments inspired suspicions of medical malfeasance with respect to people of color.

Cultural resistance to accepting or recognizing any form of depression is widespread among African Americans. Among West Africans, there is no one word for depression. Shame over the possibility of having a mental illness is common.

African Americans are more likely (15 percent versus 9 percent of whites) to represent their depression as headaches, backaches, stomachaches, and other forms of somatization (bodily manifestations of psychiatric symptoms). They are also more likely to present their symptoms as irritability, a healthy paranoia, denial, "falling out," John Henryism, and the angry black woman persona, also known as Sapphire.

Some African Americans fear that depression suggests weakness and vulnerability and a betrayal of beliefs and values. African Americans and other people of color sometimes expend great energy in making themselves appear okay when they really are not. Emotionally, it is an expensive defense.

The time from onset of symptoms to diagnosis and subsequent treatment is frequently longer than it should be. Although BPD has been recognized in all racial/ethnic groups, research efforts are underway to bring better definition to prevalence and disease presentation among different ethnic groups.

In spite of the numerous symptoms, diagnosis of bipolar illness was not made until Maya's early teens. A wise Native American teacher first concluded that Maya should be evaluated. The sensitivity, understanding, and insightfulness of this teacher cannot be overstated. It is because Ms. Joubert trusted this teacher that she agreed to have Maya tested. But Ms. Joubert readily admitted, "Had it come from anyone else, especially a white teacher, I probably would have been angry. Maya was one of only two black kids in a class of twenty-four. It would have been easy for me to think that she was being singled out because of her race."

Racial tensions often impair the cooperation and trust necessary for proper evaluation and diagnosis of mental illnesses. Several years later, a psychiatrist conducted an inpatient evaluation and diagnosed bipolar illness. This was an extremely important event. It gave Maya an opportunity for treatment and relief from her considerable psychic pain. She was more blessed than many bipolar children who go undiagnosed for years and suffer greatly as a result. Physicians are learning that bipolar illness probably evolves over time.

Diagnosis during the teen years may be easier because it more re-sembles the classic patterns of adult defined bipolar illness. The extreme swings from depression to mania (or hypomania) may be more obvious and more disruptive at school, at home, or with friends. It is more diffi-cult to attribute the behaviors to normal nuances of early child develop-ment. The adolescent is also more likely to engage in the risky, danger-ous habits of overspending (they have greater access to money) and to illegal, anti-social behaviors (stealing cars, assaulting others with little or no provocation, earning more suspensions and detentions at school secondary to violations of rules and policies). Conduct disorder be-comes a prominent diagnosis, often associated with juvenile adjudica-tion and detention. Pressured speech and racing thoughts also become more common. Psychotic symptoms (indicating mania) of hallucina-tions and delusions become much more prominent. Substance abuse disorders occur in 10 percent of child-onset bipolar disorder and in 40 percent of adolescent-onset bipolar disorder.

# X. Treatment

Treatment is the other big conundrum. Ms. Joubert clearly and elo-quently relates the family diagnosis: a lack of discipline and structure followed by the family treatment recommendation of more and better discipline. Structure, organization, and accountability help to improve and change all behaviors. And it is true that children reared in environ-ments that do not provide strong boundaries and expectations can have the irritability, aggression, anger, and inappropriate demands charac-teristic of bipolar illness. However, Ms. Joubert did understand that something other than weak parenting was affecting her child's moods, behaviors, and attitudes. Accurate diagnosis can trigger an efficient treatment outcome. Effective, long-term treatment includes biological, psychosocial, and spiritual interventions. The American Academy of Child and Adolescent Psychiatry makes the following recommendations for the diagnosis and treatment of bipolar disorder in youth:

## SCREENING

- Psychiatric assessments for children and adolescents should include screening questions for bipolar disorder.

## ASSESSMENT

- The DSM-IV criteria, including the duration criteria, should be followed when making a diagnosis of mania or hypomania in children and adolescents.
- Bipolar Disorder NOS should be used to describe youths with manic symptoms lasting hours to less than four days or for those with chronic manic-like symptoms representing their baseline level of functioning.
- Youths with suspected bipolar disorder must also be carefully evaluated for other associated problems, including suicidality, comorbid disorders (including substance abuse), psychosocial stressors, and medical problems.
- The diagnostic validity of bipolar disorder in young children has yet to be established. Caution must be taken before applying this diagnosis in preschool children.

## SOMATIC TREATMENTS

- For mania in well-defined DSM-IV-TR Bipolar I disorder, pharmacotherapy is the primary treatment.

- Most youths with Bipolar I disorder will require ongoing medication therapy to prevent relapse; some individuals will need lifelong treatment.

- Psychopharmacological interventions require baseline and follow-up symptoms, side effects (including patient's weight), and laboratory monitoring as indicated.

- For severely impaired adolescents with manic or depressive episodes in Bipolar I disorder, electroconvulsive therapy may be used if medications either are not helpful or cannot be tolerated.

## PSYCHOTHERAPEUTIC INTERVENTIONS

- Psychotherapeutic interventions are an important component of a comprehensive treatment plan (psycho-educational therapy, relapse prevention, individual psychotherapy, social and family functioning, academic and occupational functioning, and community consultation) for early onset bipolar disorder.

- The treatment of Bipolar Disorder NOS generally involves the combination of psychopharmacology with behavioral/psychosocial interventions.

Perhaps the greatest cornerstone of treatment is psycho-education.

_"I finally found another psychotherapist who connected with Maya. Dr. Ann was seeing a number of kids from Maya's high school and the school social worker had suggested her. Dr. Ann was wonderful. She was a warm and pleasant woman who used a psycho-educational approach. From the beginning she wanted Maya to understand her illness as well as she knew the cheers she recited at football games—what's_

*bipolar illness, what's cycling, what's dopamine and serotonin? Her*
*first several visits were purely educational."* —*Cassandra Joubert*

---

Although advances in neuroimaging and genetics have better defined mental disorders as legitimate illnesses, the perception that they are simply social problems that require social solutions still exists.

Education regarding bipolar disorder for the affected child/adolescent and their family is essential. Understanding that this is a legitimate, treatable illness can greatly impact treatment outcomes. Francis Bacon observed years ago that information is power. Information gives the affected person the ability to take control of their therapy by making healthy, helpful choices regarding self-support, types of therapy, choices of medication, compliance with treatment, and appropriate psycho-social interventions.

Psycho-education for the youth, parents, families, and friends becomes critical in the management of stigma. And this appears to be an even greater challenge for people and cultures of color. Ms. Joubert's struggle to engage family and friends in the management of and support for her bipolar child was huge. Relatives explained Maya's behavior on the basis of poor parenting. It seemed that no one was willing to consider the possibility of another deeper, biological issue. Without her faith to sustain her, Ms. Joubert would likely have endured even more difficulties. Families and friends of those with mental challenges would often rather that their loved one have diabetes, asthma, cancer, heart disease—anything but a mental problem. Likewise, insulin, bronchodilators, cardiac, and anti-cancer meds are acceptable; psychotropic medications are not. Never mind that cancer medication can kill the person as well as the cancer; or that steroids can negatively affect multiple organs and systems; or that anti-cholesterol medications can seriously damage the liver.

The tendency and preference is to consider mental illnesses as social problems and not as medical problems. Social problems are not so serious and it is easy to establish external blame, thereby absolving others of solutions and responsibility.

Psycho-education also allows parents to learn behavioral techniques to handle specific symptoms; Ms. Joubert herself took the initiative of providing clear boundaries for various out of control behaviors. She provided Maya with a schedule of duties related to housecleaning, car maintenance, money management, abstinence from drugs and porn, and respect for others' personal space. She provided structure in the form of expectations and consequences, which is important to establish boundaries and control impulsive, destructive behaviors.

Psychotherapy encompasses several "talk therapy" interventions. One relatively new therapy model focuses on empathic validation. Parents are able to gain insight into their negative ideas and learn techniques by which they can coach their affected child. Multiple family group treatment for bipolar youth eight to twelve years old has been effective in educating family members regarding the role of medications and effective coping strategies. Family-focused therapy for teens has been successful in developing a family-friendly environment, managing stress, accepting the disorder and recommended medications, and helping them to better personal accommodation of this disorder. Youth also learn strategies for relapse prevention.

Individual psychotherapy can address specific symptoms and concerns. It can also provide support for the often difficult to accept diagnosis of a mental disorder. There is also a role for dialectic behavioral therapy (DBT) and relapse prevention to improve long-term responses. Marsha Linehan, Ph.D. developed DBT as a therapy for borderline personality disorder. It has been examined as a therapy that can address emotional dysregulation, thought by some to be the underlying core clinical feature of bipolar disorder. Positive outcomes occur in the area of mania, depression, and negative behaviors.

# XI. Pharmacotherapy

Remember Maya's anger, irritability, violence and aggression towards her mother, frequent fights at school, rapidly changing moods with the police officer, hypersexuality, and her suicidal ideation. These are the symptoms the medications treat. Like many bipolar youth, her first diagnoses were ADHD and depression. The stimulant Adderall helped the ADHD, but the Zoloft was perhaps not the best choice for the then undiagnosed bipolar disorder.

Because bipolar illness in children so often presents as depression, major depressive disorder is often diagnosed and treated with an antidepressant. This happened to Maya—she was given Zoloft, an antidepressant of the selective serotonin reuptake inhibitors (SSRI) class of antidepressants. Her behavior began to deteriorate. As noted by Ms. Joubert, it is not clear whether the subsequent manic symptoms were secondary to the evolving course of the disorder or whether they were secondary to the "switch" phenomena.

A "switch" to hypomania/mania can occur with any antidepressant in a person who has a vulnerability to bipolar symptoms. Risk factors for antidepressant-induced mania include: prior history of mania during antidepressant therapy, evidence of rapid cycling, and presence of substance abuse. The symptoms and behaviors associated with bipolar disorder are crippling. However, the most important first step in addressing the symptoms is in addressing the problem with sleep. These youth require adequate sleep which will, to some extent, improve mood stability but not effectively enough to produce a substantial reduction in bipolar symptoms. Mood stabilizing medications will not only address the mood instability, but will also address the issue of sleep.

There are several medications available to treat bipolar disorder. Lithium has been used since 1954 for the treatment of bipolar illness. It has been shown to be very effective in the treatment of bipolar depression. Its side effect profile and the need for close monitoring of blood levels make it not widely used as a frontline medication by most physicians. Many people in the manic phase do not respond and its onset of action is longer than other medication choices. It has been approved for use in children thirteen years old and older.

Lithium has been uniquely effective in the prevention of suicide and suicide attempts. Studies show that the suicide rate drops to nearly zero in suicidal persons taking lithium. Though highly effective for some, there may be more side effects in African Americans.

Other medications used to treat bipolar disorder are known as mood stabilizers. Mood stabilizer implies the ability of the medicine to prevent extremes of mood, either high or low. An evenness of mood is referred to as euthymia. An agent is a mood stabilizer if it effectively treats acute manic and depressive symptoms and maintains mood stability (prophylaxis of manic and depressive symptoms in bipolar disorder). There are basically two groups of mood stabilizer. One group is the anticonvulsants and the other is the atypical antipsychotics.

For reasons that are poorly understood, some anticonvulsants appear to be effective. These include Depakote, Tegretol, Trileptal, and Lamotrigine. Depakote is an anticonvulsant that has been shown to be especially effective in the treatment of rapid-cycling or mixed states of bipolar illness. However, it must be carefully monitored when prescribed for young females. A possible side effect for some females under twenty is polycystic ovarian syndrome (PCOS). In the STEP-BD study, 10.5 percent of a study sample developed this side effect.

Atypical antipsychotic medications (also known as second generation antipsychotics) have also received Federal Drug Administration (FDA) approval for treatment of bipolar mania. Reportedly, widespread support for the use of this group of medications exists because they have a greater safety profile and require less invasive management and monitoring of the patient. Patients tend to respond fairly rapidly to this class of medications. Hence, physicians often perceive it as a first line treatment for bipolar disorder. These include Risperdol, Seroquel, Geodon, Abilify, and Zyprexa. The best medications for treatment of BPD remain under investigation. The recommendation currently is that youth receive both a mood stabilizer and an atypical antipsychotic.

Every medication, regardless of type, requires close monitoring. The child/adolescent psychiatrist should evaluate bipolar youth at least monthly and conduct all necessary lab studies. Evaluations of glucose, cholesterol, and triglycerides should occur after a fasting period for more accurate measurements of those chemistries. Yearly physical exams and regular checking of waist size and blood pressure are also important. Studies on the effectiveness and safety of psychotropic medications in the treatment of pediatric BPD are limited. Actually, there are few medications in any category that have undergone scientific scrutiny and validation for use in children.

Long-term outcomes of treatment of child or adolescent onset bipolar disorder are not well documented, although chronic functional impairment and treatment resistance into adulthood has been noted. One recent study followed adolescents with bipolar disorder for a year after hospital discharge. Only one third adhered fully with their prescribed medication schedule. Poor medication adherence, co-occurring attention deficit disorder, anxiety disorders, disruptive behavior disorders, and lower socioeconomic disorders predicted poor syndrome recovery. Syndromic recurrence was more likely if there was a co-occurring alcohol use disorder, no psychotherapy, and treatment regimens that included antidepressants. Boys were more likely than girls to have symptomatic recovery. Overall, reduction in symptoms and functional recovery were low.

Failure to properly diagnose and treat this disorder can result in increased hospitalizations, suicide attempts, financial burden, dangerous and life-threatening behaviors, and substance abuse. Furthermore, there is a growing body of research into diseases of the mind that suggests delays in treatment can allow for greater brain deterioration. The new research also suggests that delays in treatment seem to impair the ability of the central nervous system to respond to treatment when it is initiated.

Hospitalization may be a necessary element for diagnosis. More targeted and efficient treatment did not occur for Maya until a psychiatric hospitalization. Because of hospital costs and inadequate hospital resources for these youth, hospitalization can be difficult and elusive. Long-term hospitalization in the form of residential treatment is sometimes necessary for long-term stabilization. As Ms. Joubert found out, this is an expensive option. Thousands of dollars are not easily accessible for most. Cost has made this a treatment option primarily for well-to-do whites. Youth of color are often relegated to the juvenile justice system. The school recommendation that Maya go to the local juvenile detention center is the more common option and outcome for children of color.

A variety of possible effective treatments exist for any disorder. Perhaps the best, most effective treatment for Maya was her mother.

Without her, Maya might not be here today. One can never underestimate the healing and calming power of love, protection, patience, and boundaries. As one follows the path of Maya's life and of her illness, the one constant clearly has been Ms. Joubert.

# XII. The Caregiver Burden

---

*"This whole thing was starting to take its toll on me. I was orchestrating her life day in and out—communicating with the school, shepherding her through therapy, managing her psychiatrist appointments and her meds; all the while trying to keep my male child focused on his college career. I was paying his tuition, taking his late night phone calls; my life was consumed with everything except anything for me. And it was beginning to take its toll. Somehow, I put it all on cruise control and with God as my co-pilot, kept on managing everything. My subscription to the* Upper Room *continued to provide me daily e-prayers, which kept me lifted up and sane."* —*Cassandra Joubert*

---

As one reads the narrative and understands the sacrifices and stresses of Ms. Joubert's life, it is impossible not to wonder who supports her. Caregiver burden is often overlooked, but is a critical aspect of treatment of mentally ill persons.

It is no accident that the families of people with mental illness often abandon and reject them. Numerous studies have documented the consequences of being a primary caretaker in these situations. Most would agree that managing mental disabilities is far more challenging than managing physical disabilities. There are fewer treatment resources, and the disease course is more unpredictable. Those who have not been in Ms. Joubert's position can easily trivialize, minimize, and dismiss the force of this illness and the impact on the family. Those who have had the experience have a very different reality in terms of mental disabilities. Some family members of bipolar manic children and adolescents talk of having to take turns staying up through the night to monitor the sometimes endangering and unpredictable behaviors.

In an interview, Ms. Joubert talked about the some of the emotional struggles she endured. She admits that some unresolved issues still exist deep within her emotions that are still too painful to address.

---

*"I look at myself today and I wonder where I went. I use to like to be around people. I use to be involved in my community. I use to be concerned about issues. At some point I became aware that if I was going to make it through this, I had to give up everything else.*

*I didn't even date for five years after my ex-husband and I broke up. My relationship with my child was so intense and so demanding and so overwhelming that I couldn't manage another intimate relationship. I had to say, this is what I'm giving up and I have to do it. Many times, I got to a point of hopelessness.*

*I came to the conclusion that it might be like this forever.*

*I considered the possibility that it would just be me and my child, and that I would just have to take care of her. I had been heavily involved my church, chairwoman of the vestry and many other activities. I stopped going to church, because in church you have to say "hi" to people, fraternize. I didn't have the energy for that. Another reason I stopped going to church is that whenever I went, all I did was cry the whole time. I would weep uncontrollably. I lost faith in a lot of stuff.*

*The first time I sat foot back in church was about a year and a half after she was diagnosed and treated. I had been out of the church for about four years.*

*I had two or three good girlfriends who could help me. But mostly, I put myself on cruise control, just going through the motions for years, just knowing I had to do this or arrange that, or resolve the other.*

*If I had adopted the attitude that I can just let God handle it, I don't think things would have turned out as well as they did. I was totally devoted to her. You know what they say, 'God helps those who help themselves.'"* —**Cassandra Joubert**

---

Serious mental disorders can bring caregivers to their knees. This is more likely to occur when mental health resources, family, and friends are inaccessible and unsupportive. Shame, guilt, confusion, powerlessness, fear, anger, isolation, and exhaustion become bedfellows. In addition, the caregiver is often trying to meet the needs of other children, a husband or spouse, a job. Every day is unpredictable and challenging. But some useful guidelines can help caregivers manage what at times must seem unmanageable.

The caregiver must:

- Research, get second opinions, and learn as much as possible about the disorder.

- Identify an accomplished, knowledgeable team of bipolar experts that can provide effective treatment planning. This may include child/adolescent psychiatrists, cognitive-behavioral therapists, and psychotherapists.

- Determine your child's special education needs.

- When possible, rely on family, friends, and community resources, such as church members, to supervise or care for the child to allow time for your personal interests or brief getaways.

- Resist the temptation to do everything and to be all things to all people.

- Develop connections with local bipolar advocacy groups. They can provide help and information, and be a source of support and empathy for both the child and the caregiver.

- Be open to help from individual and family therapy and pastoral counseling.

- Take care of yourself; exercise, eat well, and try relaxation techniques such as yoga and meditation.

- Seek spirituality.

- Don't be afraid to ask for help.

# SECTION THREE:

## A Cause to Advocate

by Linda Thompson Adams, DrPH, RN, FAAN

*"For nothing is fixed, forever and forever and forever, it is not fixed;
the earth is always shifting, the light is always changing, the sea does
not cease to grind down rock. Generations do not cease to be born,
and we are responsible to them because we are the only witnesses
they have. The sea rises, the light fails, lovers cling to each other,
and children cling to us. The moment we cease to hold each other,
the sea engulfs us and the light goes out."* —James Baldwin

# I. Introduction

Ms. Joubert would have seen the red flags had she known what they looked like. Instead all she saw was the color of a mother's love, fear, and concern. No mother should have to endure such a personal and preventable agony, and certainly not alone, without the help or understanding of family, community, or society as a whole. And no child should have to abandon youthful bliss for a shadowy, lonely, terrifying journey.

No one would wish such a fate on an adult. To watch it happen to an innocent child is unthinkable. And yet, for decades, thousands of children have been born into that shadowy existence, chased and taunted by things inside their heads, things that no one—parent, sibling, playmate, teacher, preacher—seemed able to see, hear, or understand. Until now.

Now we are beginning to recognize and understand that frightful thing. We are beginning to learn how to keep it at bay, how to push it behind a protective barricade, how to thrive despite it, how to demand the help that is every person's right, and how to educate others so that we can rid ourselves, our loved ones, and friends of needless suffering.

Ms. Joubert had to learn on her own, through trial and error, progress and setback. Even today, with Maya entering young adulthood, there is still more to learn, more battles to fight, because the battle with bipolar disorder never ends. People just keep getting smarter about how to fight it.

Every parent, teacher, friend, relative, physician, mental health-care provider, juvenile justice professional, child welfare professional, and community or spiritual leader can help. It just takes enough care and determination to understand the disorder, and learn what to look for, what to look out for, where to go, who to talk to, and what to insist upon.

# II. What Do Children Need?

The needs of children could be broadly defined as the need for protection. A child should be protected from anything that can harm healthy growth and development. Most of the time, this requires a fight. Whether it is an adult fighting to be a good parent, a community leader fighting for a quality education system, or a politician fighting budget cuts in children's programs, only an honest commitment at the national, local, community, and family levels will assure the protection of children.

According to the most recent U.S. Census, in 2003, there were seventy-three million children ages newborn to seventeen living in the United States. That's seventy-three million infants, children, and adolescents who need protection. Of those, 60 percent were white, 19 percent were Hispanic, and 16 percent African American. By 2020, the child population is expected to reach eighty million, and African American percentages are expected to remain third behind whites and Hispanics.

The needs of the children are many. On all levels, the detrimental circumstances faced by many children, particularly those of ethnic minorities, include startling rates of obesity, infant mortality, adolescent deaths, undiagnosed mental illness and child abuse, inadequate education and healthcare systems, poor family structure, and low economic status. In the United States, our policymakers, systems, and institutions like to think of themselves as protectors of children, and they are in many ways.

Beginning with the Constitution of the United States, which guarantees every American certain inalienable rights as well as civil rights, there are numerous federal and state laws, policies, regulations, programs, and practices designed to protect children. There are laws against child abuse, laws mandating education, laws prohibiting child labor, laws governing the rights of children in the juvenile justice system, and programs that assist with healthcare, nutrition, and shelter. Still, numerous reports, studies, and experts have found that the nation's complex system of child protection is increasingly inadequate to meet the needs of significant numbers of children in general and minority, poor, and African American children in particular.

Each year since 1997, the Federal Interagency Forum on Child and Family Statistics has produced America's Children: Key National Indicators of Well Being. America's Children 2005, found that only 35 percent of African American children lived with two married parents, compared to 65 percent of Hispanic children and 77 percent of white children. In 2003, 34 percent of African American children lived in poverty, compared to 30 percent of Hispanic children and 10 percent of white children.

African American youth were likely to be victims of serious violent crime at rates only slightly higher than whites, but three times as likely as other youth to be victims of violence.

White children were more likely than African American or Hispanic children to have very good or excellent general health. Also in 2003, 89 percent of all children were covered by health insurance at some point during the year, and another 11 percent or 8.4 million had no health insurance at all during the year.

The Annie E. Casey Foundation's 2003-2004 Key Indicators of Child Well-Being also found, among African American children, substantially higher rates of low-birth weight, infant mortality, child and teen deaths, and higher percentages of teens who were neither working nor in school.

In recent years, mental health has been identified as one of the most neglected areas of a child's well-being. Significant investigations and studies of children's mental health reported appalling findings about the numbers of children suffering from mental illnesses, the inadequacies of systems in place to serve these children and the devastating results for children and families.

*"The burden of suffering experienced by children with mental health needs and their families has created a health crisis in this country. Growing numbers of children are suffering needlessly because their emotional, behavioral, and developmental needs are not being met by those very institutions which were explicitly created to take care of them." (Foreword: David Satcher, MD, PhD, Assistant Secretary for Health and Surgeon General. Report of the Surgeon General's Conference on Children's Mental*

*Health: A National Action Agenda. Department of Health and Human Services. January 3, 2001.)*

*"America's mental health service delivery system is in shambles ... There are so many programs operating under such different rules that it is often impossible for families and consumers to find the care that they urgently need ... As a result, too many Americans suffer needless disability, and millions of dollars are spent unproductively in a dysfunctional service system that cannot deliver the treatments that work so well ... The Commission has heard from families whose children could not get an accurate diagnosis for years ... All of the problems are disproportionately worse for children who are ethnic and racial minorities" (DHHS, 2001).*

# III.  Who Should Protect Our Children?

*"To nourish children and raise them against odds is in anytime, anyplace, more valuable than to fix bolts in cars or design nuclear weapons."* **—Marilyn French**

Ideally, society as a whole would protect the children, because no culture, no nation, no species can survive without the continuous cycle of life that begins with each birth. In the area of mental health, stakeholders should include educators, healthcare providers and professionals, social workers, community and spiritual leaders, elected officials, local and federal regulatory agencies, advocacy groups, and most importantly parents.

No one has a more compelling motive for the well-being of children than the parent.

As we have learned from Ms. Joubert's story, mental illness is not choosy about socio-economic status. Here is a mother who throughout her life was well-educated, well-employed, and well-insured and yet she faced a daunting uphill battle to find help for her child and her family. Many parents don't have a fraction of the resources Ms. Joubert had at her disposal and for them the challenge can seem insurmountable. They, more than others, need the guidance, help, and support of all stakeholders to enable them to help their children.

Today there are more single-parent homes, poor mothers raising children, limited or no paternal influence, and uneducated parents with little or no income potential.

There are the added pressures of trying to do it all on one's own, not having the resources to help, not knowing where to find the resources, or not knowing that the resources even exist. Economically challenged parents tend to experience increased levels of stress and anxiety related to their situation—poverty stricken, under-educated, and isolated, they are headed for a state of hopelessness. This state of mind can spill over into the home environment and adversely affect the healthy development of children.

It has been said that whatever happens in American society affects African Americans twice as much. The African American experience is always qualified by the impact of living in a nation and a society that routinely treats people differently based on skin color. Whether it's in employment, housing, politics, education, or healthcare, African Americans, more than any other group, generally have to struggle against the complicating factor of discrimination. African Americans are also disproportionately represented among the poor, the homeless, the unemployed, the uninsured, the incarcerated, and in neighborhoods where violence, substance abuse, and crime are prevalent.

Some researchers believe that these high-needs populations are at greater risk for developing mental illnesses.

This is a burden that too often causes African Americans to sacrifice their physical and mental health; to give up, accept the status quo, and forget their own power. They forget how their ancestors struggled with far less and through times when even the law was not on their side. Circumstances become mechanisms of control. Children not only suffer at the hands of adults who exhibit these behaviors, they internalize those same attitudes and carry them forward to the next generation.

Children are the innocents of the world. They are born virtually helpless and totally dependent upon adults for food, water, shelter, and clothing. But those are only the basic human needs necessary for survival. To thrive, children need to be mentally and developmentally healthy.

As difficult as it can be at times, African American parents can and must become fierce advocates and informed consumers of mental healthcare for children. But parents should not be left to bear this responsibility alone. The systems in place to support families and children have a legal and moral responsibility to assure that every child who needs mental healthcare gets that care in the most efficient and effective manner possible. But as the Surgeon General's report of 1999 and the President's New Freedom Commission on Mental Health, October 2002, showed, the systems and safety nets are failing.

*"A fragmented services system is one of several systemic barriers impeding the delivery of effective mental health care. Our interim report describes other problems, including our failure to serve those with the most serious*

*illnesses, our failure to intervene early in childhood, and our Nation's failure to recognize mental health care as a national priority ... The reality is that the mental health system looks more like a maze than a coordinated system of care." (President's New Freedom Commission on Mental Health October 2002).*

The nation's research archives are filled with studies and reports on the failures of the mental healthcare system. There are thousands of stories just like Ms. Joubert's—parents wandering helplessly through a haze of confusion about what is wrong with their child and what to do about it. Like physical health, mental health touches every aspect of a child's life. There are many people within our various systems and institutions who come into contact with children and, for a variety of reasons that will be discussed later, miss opportunities to identify and address mental health needs. Left unrecognized and untreated, the child's condition progresses to more serious levels, impacting every facet of the child's growth and development.

A preschool worker or an elementary school teacher will recognize when a child has a cold or a rash, and will inform the parent that the child needs medical attention. But a child exhibiting emotional or behavior problems might simply be labeled as undisciplined or a slow learner.

Most children visit a primary care physician at various intervals. While some physicians might recognize that a child may be suffering from emotional or behavioral problems and refer the child to a mental health specialist, follow through by the parent might not occur for many reasons, including financial barriers and social stigma. In other cases, cultural incompetence in primary care can lead to misdiagnosis or missed diagnosis, particularly of African American children.

One of the most insidious manifestations of the failure of the mental healthcare system is the overrepresentation of mentally ill or emotionally disturbed children in the juvenile justice system. Their untreated conditions have left them susceptible to behaviors that are interpreted as criminal rather than psychological. In all of these instances, African American and other minority children fare the worse.

America, more than any other country, has the resources to provide its children and families with mental healthcare services that support a full and productive life. Every stakeholder, from parents, to healthcare professionals, to educators and researchers, has a role to play. If we are to protect and save our children, each stakeholder must gain the tools and insights necessary to remove the barriers that separate, confuse, and mishandle the very people the systems are charged with serving.

There are well-defined steps to gaining the skills necessary to navigate the current systems and to implement improvements and find new approaches. For purposes of this discussion of providing better mental healthcare for African American children suffering from bipolar disorder in particular, and mental and emotional challenges in general, we will divide the stakeholders into two groups: consumers and providers. Consumers are parents and family units who have a child in need of services. Providers are all the systems, organizations, and institutions that offer services or support for children and families and are well-positioned to advocate for change.

# IV. Parents as Consumers

Any parent can be a good consumer of mental healthcare if provided with the knowledge and armed with the commitment to seek the best services for the child. With our systems in disarray, a parent has to be especially prepared for difficulty and frustration. But the well-being of children is worth all the hardship. African American parents and families usually face additional layers of difficulty, based in part on cultural practices and on an array of bias and disparity in society's systems and institutions.

It has been documented that race, ethnicity, and culture can influence the diagnosis and treatment children receive. One expert found that African American children are more likely to be referred for conduct problems or to the juvenile justice system than for psychiatric treatment (U.S. Public Health Service, Report of the Surgeon General Conference on Children's Mental Health: A National Action Agenda. Washington, DC: Department of Health and Human Services, 2000).

But nothing will change unless these issues are faced and challenged no matter how painful or difficult the process. It starts with each of us. For Ms. Joubert, the courage to share her story is an act of caring for African American families and children who, regardless of their socio-economic status, can be victimized by lack of their own knowledge and understanding, and by unresponsive and inadequate systems of care.

The following are some basic starting points that will help parents become informed consumers and shrewd negotiators when seeking mental health services for their children.

- Gain awareness of the prevalence of mental illness and disorder;
- Pay attention to your child's development and behaviors;
- Examine your parenting style;
- Overcome the stigma;
- Seek treatment and support;
- Monitor your child's treatment, challenge the providers;
- Know your rights;
- Become an advocate for systematic change.

# V. You Are Not Alone

Most people have no idea of how many African American children suffer from bipolar disorder or other mental illnesses, disorders, and behavioral and emotional difficulties. Although numbers exist for all adults, national surveys to determine the prevalence among children have only recently become a priority.

In a January 2001 press release from the U.S. Department of Health and Human Services, the U.S. Surgeon General declared, "In the United States, one in ten children and adolescents suffer from mental illness severe enough to cause some level of impairment."

America's Children 2005 for the first time surveyed one aspect of children's mental health by asking parents whether their children had "definite or severe difficulties with emotions, concentration, behavior, or being able to get along with other people," all of which can be indicators of bipolar disorder. Based on parental reports, the survey showed that 5 percent of children aged four to seventeen, or 2.7 million, did exhibit such difficulties.

Experts are only recently beginning to acknowledge the occurrence of bipolar disorder in children and actual statistics for African American children and children in general are difficult to determine. However the National Institutes of Mental Health (NIMH) estimates that 5.7 million people or 2.6 percent of the U.S. population age eighteen or older are affected by bipolar disorder in a given year (National Institutes of Mental Health Fact Sheet, 2006).

NIMH also estimates that at least 26 percent of Americans age eighteen or older, fifty-seven million people, have some diagnosable mental disorder in any given year. The point is that mental illness is very common in America and it affects all racial, ethnic, and socio-economic groups. What African American parents need to know is that for their children, disparities exist in diagnosis and treatment, as well as in the attitudes and responses of service providers. This is only one of many challenges to seeking services for children.

# VI. Know Your Child

From the time her daughter was an infant, Ms. Joubert had a sense of unease. All babies are different, so the contrasts between her firstborn son and her new infant daughter seemed of little consequence. As the years passed, Ms. Joubert was drawn deeper and deeper into the consequences of undiagnosed or misdiagnosed mental disorder. It is important for parents to be aware of the thin line between normal childhood behavior issues and the symptoms of more serious problems.

Only in the past decade, mental health professionals have began to consider that infants and young children could suffer from bipolar disorder. Even now, many professionals still believe the average age for onset of the disorder is young adulthood. Still enough evidence of pediatric disorder has been gathered to prompt an intense focus on diagnosing and treating young children.

Recognizing bipolar disorder in children is difficult even for professionals. Parents are at an even greater disadvantage. Confronted by negative behavior reports from teachers, relatives, and friends, parents can be convinced that their children are just plain bad. But a parent knows the child better than anyone and must question assessments made by teachers, the juvenile justice system, physicians, and others.

Children experience troublesome behaviors for many reasons. A child exposed to violence can suffer long-term psychological damage resulting in aggressive behavior, or depressed moods. Poor nutrition or inadequate prenatal care can lead to learning difficulties. A sexually abused child can exhibit depression or heightened sexual interests. All of those circumstances require immediate attention, but the services needed are different for children suffering from severe mental disorders.

Some of the distinct signs that a child may have bipolar disorder, such as mood swings, sleeplessness, behaviors that include running away, and uncharacteristic sexuality, are discussed at length in Section Two. What is important for parents to understand is that if they know their children and have no explanation for why a child would exhibit such behaviors, they should consider the presence of a mental disorder or mental illness.

While judging what is really causing certain child behaviors is sometimes difficult, it is important to include mental disorders among the possibilities. As with any other illness, early detection is key. Untreated, children with mental disorders can fail repeatedly in school, or eventually drop out. They can be drawn into a lifetime of progressively detrimental behavior like drug abuse, criminal conduct, and sexual promiscuity. The physical and psychological damage from these behaviors is clear.

Various studies and reports estimate that large percentages of children who engage in criminal acts suffer from a mental illness or disorder. According to the *Key Issues National Center for Mental Health and Juvenile Justice*:

Key Issue 2: The prevalence of mental disorder among youth in the juvenile justice system is two to three times higher than among youth in the general population.

While the research base on this issue is very much still developing, existing research suggests that most youth in the juvenile justice system, anywhere from 70 to 100%, have a diagnosable mental disorder. Approximately one out of five (20 percent) has a serious mental disorder.

One of the most disturbing examples of misdiagnosed and untreated mental disorders in children is the startling statistics on detentions in the juvenile justice system. Thousands of children are being held in detention centers simply because there are no services available to treat their mental illnesses. This abysmal situation was documented in Incarceration of Youth Who Are Waiting for Community Mental Health Services in the United States, a special report from the United States House of Representatives Committee on Government Reform – Minority Staff Special Investigations Division, July 2004, prepared for Representative Henry A. Waxman and Senator Susan Collins.

Based on responses from three-fourths of all juvenile detention centers in the U.S. (January to June 2003), the Waxman-Collins investigation found that in thirty-three states, children as young as seven years old who had committed no crime, were being held until mental health services could be found. Many of the facilities reported suicide attempts and attacks against others among these youths.

The investigation, citing a 2003 report from the U.S. General Accounting Office, also reported that in order to get mental health services for their children, thousands of families give up custody to governmental agencies.

# VII. Examining Our Parenting Methods

For the most part, African American parents are unlikely to study child-rearing theories when it comes to raising their children. Certainly, in Ms. Joubert's day, it was unheard of to listen to a child's reason for disobedience or to administer a time out instead of a spanking. To many African Americans, Dr. Spock, who popularized alternative child-rearing, was a fool with a parenting philosophy designed for rich or permissive white parents and upper-class black parents who were "trying to act white."

After all, the standard of strict discipline had protected children for generations and was steeped in centuries of the African American experience in a racist society. To let a black child out into the world without strict parameters could be disastrous physically and psychologically. Even today, African American children, particularly males, regardless of their upbringing, education, or economic status are often profiled by whites as obviously up to no good. The expression "Driving While Black," which grew out of the ongoing tendency of white law enforcement officers to stop African Americans, feeds the tendency of black parents to protect their children by exercising strict control. This is understandable, but as much as African American parents want to resist raising their children by someone else's book, there is value in considering some of the more useful aspects of child-rearing options.

Researchers have labeled the parenting styles based on the levels of demand and responsiveness in the parent. The resulting four types of parenting—authoritarian, authoritative, indulgent, and uninvolved—are believed to result in distinct development patterns in the children. Indulgent or uninvolved parenting would logically be the least desired or recommended form.

Authoritarian parenting, where strict, unquestioned control and discipline are practiced with little consideration of the child's personality, opinion, or individual needs, might seem wise and responsible. While the child of the authoritarian parent will generally have fewer behavioral problems, research has shown that this child will also perform only moderately in school, have undeveloped social skills, low self esteem, and be at higher risk for depression.

On the other hand, an authoritative parenting style accompanied by strong parental monitoring proved beneficial in fostering positive adaptation, responsibility, organization, and achievement in minority youth. In fact, it was believed to be the most effective method of parenting in light of the high-risk environment. In conjunction with this, a positive supportive environment with a strong element of control was found to promote the development of black children.

Ms. Joubert was at first conflicted by the rules of parenting that had been passed down from her parents and grandparents and the alternative parenting style that modern experts said would work best for her bipolar child. The more she read and learned directly from the interactions with Maya, the more she traded her own need for absolute control for the flexibility that would be best for Maya.

No one can demand that parents adopt a particular method of child rearing, but the suggestion of taking an objective look at recommendations from child development experts is worthy of consideration.

# VIII.  Abandon the Stigma

*My first and only bump with the LRC came soon after Maya started attending the center. Observing Maya's uneven performance—good some days, not so good on others—the LRC teacher said she thought that Maya might be bipolar. I looked at her in shock.  I thought to myself, "You've only known my child for a week and you are already labeling her?" I was really angry with her, but said nothing.*

*She went on to say that her daughter was bipolar, and then a light bulb went off within me. Oh, I thought, just because your daughter is bipolar, you think every kid that has challenges must have the same problem. I really resented her for diagnosing Maya. After all, she wasn't a psychologist or therapist. She was just another teacher like the rest of them. It wasn't until a year or more later that I realized that when someone is the parent of an emotionally impaired child—living with them, struggling with them, and worrying about them day in and day out—they know more about mental illness than all the psychologists and psychiatrists combined!*

There are many reasons why a parent can't or won't pursue a child's mental health diagnosis and treatment. Often a family lacks financial resources or adequate healthcare. But many studies have found that there is another factor at work—that of the stigma surrounding mental illness.

Mental illness is still often seen as some kind of genetic flaw or weakness in character or upbringing. Numerous reports have concluded that the burden of stigma and a lack of knowledge about the nature of mental illness prevent many people from seeking treatment.

The stigma is deeply rooted in society. People suffering from mental illness have been subjected to the unkind and insensitive attitudes of others. They have been discriminated against in the community and the workplace, labeled as odd or strange, and feared as violent or dangerous. For centuries, many of the institutions established to treat the mentally ill were places of torment and ill treatment, perpetuated by unqualified and untrained staff and lack of medical knowledge of the causes of mental illness. Even with the advancement of medical science and treatment options, the stigma for many is difficult to overcome.

According to a 1999 Fact Sheet from the U.S. Surgeon General's Office, African Americans overall suffer from mental illness at rates similar to other groups, but show higher rates for specific diseases, for example phobias, and somatization or psychosomatic illnesses. In either instance, African Americans are less likely than whites to seek treatment. This reluctance has many causes, but includes the stigma surrounding mental illness.

Some experts have concluded that African Americans often rely on family love and care or religious beliefs to help their mentally ill, rather than expose themselves to possible public scrutiny by seeking professional care.

It is time to set aside those misconceptions and embrace the truth that mental illness is not a weakness or deficiency. The human body is amazing and complex. Physical health and mental health work together to assure a well-adjusted and functioning human being, and each is equally susceptible to disruption and breakdown.

There is nothing odd or strange about it. A person should be no more ashamed or reluctant to seek mental healthcare for a mental illness than they would be to seek a pain reliever for a headache. Children cannot be expected to seek treatment on their own and parents cannot wait for attitudes to change. More efforts are needed to educate and sensitize parents and the public on childhood mental illness so that stigma and other social barriers can be removed. In the meantime, parents have to make a leap of faith across decades of misinformation and find the strength to face the issue and seek the help their children need.

# IX. Seek Treatment

*"My message to Americans is this: If you, or a loved one, are experiencing what you believe might be the symptoms of a mental disorder, do not hesitate to seek effective treatment now." —David Satcher, MD, PhD, U.S. Surgeon General*

Several studies have indicated that far too many people suffering from a mental disorder go untreated. In one finding, the Centers for Disease Control (CDC) estimates that only half of the adults in the U.S. with a diagnosable mental disorder get treatment and only one third of the 13.7 million children who have a mental health need actually gets help. These are disturbing statistics because they indicate that millions of adults and children live day to day in turmoil, while treatments are available for most mental disorders.

Suicide is one of the most devastating consequences of untreated mental disorders. As the eighth leading cause of death in the U.S., suicide is the unanswerable plea for help and an outcome that can torment those left behind. The CDC reports that 80-90 percent of suicides are by people with a mental disorder.

The risk of suicide or other negative outcomes underscore the urgency for families to set aside the stigma, overcome the denial, and focus on getting treatment for loved ones in need. Start somewhere, even if it is simply calling a trusted friend or relative and saying, "I think something's wrong." Another option is to seek advice from a minister or someone in the spiritual community who knows you and your family.

Those are just beginning points. The most important step is to seek professional help. You can start with the child's primary care physician or pediatrician, who can make a referral to a mental healthcare professional.

There are many choices to make when seeking professional help for a child with mental health needs. Just trying to get the correct diagnosis can mean a cycle of hope and disappointment because, as with some physical illnesses, finding what's wrong with a mind can be complex. Parents must be prepared to take on the arduous task of learning as much as possible about the illness and the kinds of treatment available. This is a time to ask a lot of questions and to make sure that the answers provide the knowledge needed to make an informed decision. Information that will help explain your options should be provided by the healthcare professional, but can also be obtained on the Internet, from psychology and psychiatry departments at colleges and universities in your community, and from public health institutions in your state or county. Try every available source.

Even with a broad range of information, African American parents face additional challenges. Historically, as with most American institutions, the African American experience in the medical profession comes with an unsettling past, steeped in distrust and disparity. The history goes far beyond the Tuskegee Syphilis Study that began in 1932 and lasted for forty years. Nearly four hundred black men were denied treatment for syphilis so that researchers could study the effects of the disease on the human body. Many of those enrolled in the study died. In other cases, the untreated disease was spread to spouses and children. When the science-fiction-like experiment was exposed, it was more than disturbing. The experiment was another piece of cruel evidence that African Americans were considered expendable and less than human, even by healthcare professionals sworn to heal and preserve life.

Even before the Tuskegee experiment, and certainly after, African Americans were discriminated against in many ways by the nation's healthcare institutions. Like every other system in America, hospitals, clinics, and doctor's offices were separate and unequal. Medical schools and nursing colleges denied enrollment to African Americans aspiring to enter the healthcare profession. This discrimination gave rise to black institutions of higher learning, many of which still exist today. Even as these institutions graduated doctors and nurses, many could not find employment in the major white hospitals or physicians' offices.

As segregation eased, and African American patients were allowed to seek treatment at the facility of their choice, another interesting phenomenon developed, one that could only be described as the result of the lie of black inferiority, propaganda, and eroded self-esteem. Many African Americans adopted the belief that African American healthcare professionals were not as qualified as white professionals. Many abandoned the black doctors and nurses who had cared for them, choosing white professionals who they believed to be smarter or better trained.

But an interesting conversion is taking place in many segments of the African American community. Today, many African American patients actively seek African American physicians. The uncertainty of some African Americans about the health care they receive in a mostly white field is probably linked as much to the discrimination they have faced in all facets of life in America, as it is to revelations such as the Tuskegee experiment.

In reality, healthcare professionals of all races are a dedicated group of people who approach each patient regardless of race with the intent of providing the best care they know. But what they know is exactly the point in question.

Throughout history, most medical research has been geared to the majority population for a variety of reasons. One, whites are the majority population in this country and therefore have larger numbers from which research participants can be drawn. Two, African Americans for a variety of reasons, including the mistrust and lack of knowledge about the value of medical research, have been reluctant to volunteer for research studies. This means the base of knowledge used to treat physical and mental illness has few footnotes on the development and treatment of disease in African Americans.

This lack of research means no one can say with certainty whether certain cultural nuances or physical or environmental considerations should be made when diagnosing and treating illness in African Americans. After all, for decades African Americans have fought for the right to be treated the same as everyone else. But science links more and more environmental and cultural influences to mental and physical health.

There is evidence that African Americans metabolize medications differently than other groups. Some mental health experts now believe that the stresses of discrimination and racism can lead to some forms of mental illness. The majority of African Americans live in urban areas subjected to higher levels of poverty, pollution, crime, noise, and other factors that can also impact mental and physical health. In addition, some studies have shown that patient trust of the healthcare provider can influence health outcomes. A patient who does not trust the physician may hold back information that could be important to treatment or they may question the physician's interest or sincerity.

Should these factors be considered when diagnosing and treating African Americans and other minority or ethnic groups? More and more the answer is yes. It is a relatively new concept called "cultural competence," and this concept means more than just the race of the healthcare provider. It would be improper and incorrect to suggest that patient and physician have to be of the same race or ethnicity to get the best outcome. Quite the contrary, cultural competence means sensitizing healthcare professionals to the differences in their patients through diversity in research, education, attitudes, and community intervention and education. Several well-qualified panels of experts have identified approaches to achieving cultural competence and their recommendations will be discussed at greater length later in these chapters.

It will take years to correct the inequities in this nation's healthcare services. For example, an African American parent seeking an African American mental healthcare provider for a child would face some difficulty, since only about 2 percent of psychiatrists and psychologists in the U.S. are African American (African American Community Mental Health Fact Sheet; National Alliance on Mental Illness, Multicultural Action Center). In the meantime, the millions of children and adults suffering from untreated mental illnesses cannot wait for the system to catch up on all issues of healthcare. There are treatments right now that work and can be used to improve the health and life experiences of any patient.

> *"It is abundantly clear that good treatment is preferable to no treatment at all . . . Every person, regardless of race or ethnicity, should seek help if they have a mental health problem or symptoms of a mental disorder ... At present, members of minority groups may experience limited availability of, and access to, culturally sensitive treatments. With time, access to these services should improve as a result of awareness of this problem and the courses of action identified in this Supplement ... In the meantime, anyone who needs help must hear a simple, yet resounding, message of hope: Treatment works and recovery is possible." (Executive Summary: Mental Health: Culture, Race and Ethnicity; A Supplement to Mental Health: A Report of the Surgeon General, 1999.)*

# X. Monitor Your Child's Treatment

Science has not yet caught up with the diagnosis and treatment of bipolar disorder in children. Most of the medications used to treat bipolar disorder were formulated for adults, but are also used for children. All are very powerful drugs and a child's medication must be closely monitored to see whether it is helping or hurting, and what, if any, side effects occur.

This can be a challenge for parents. Many times people assume that because a medication was prescribed by a physician it must be the best thing, and it actually is most of the time. Still, there are many factors to consider when assuring that your child is getting the best treatment.

Ms. Joubert watched her daughter do well on some medications and not so well on others. Part of the initial difficulty was getting the correct diagnosis of her daughter's illness, which took many years. The right treatment for the wrong illness could have serious physical and psychological impacts on a child.

In addition, the research into the diagnosis and treatment of bipolar in children is still very new. The medical field does not have nearly enough information; and, in fact, there are varying theories on which medications, therapies, and approaches work best. So even with the correct diagnosis of bipolar, finding the proper treatment can take weeks, months, or longer. This can be a trying time for parents. Patience and determination are essential.

Parents anxious to help their children must ask questions, insist on full explanations of what to expect, and, most importantly, keep good notes or other documentation of what medications their children are taking and what effects occur. Get comfortable with talking to medical professionals. Parents may not be medically trained, but common sense and knowing your child go a long way.

Treatment for bipolar children is always a balancing act between so many elements: medication, therapies, hospitalizations, family environment, and relationships. Results can be intense and unpredictable.

That's why observation and documentation are very important in monitoring the child's progress and setbacks. Start a diary or notebook where everything can be written down in one place daily, or at whatever intervals work best. Keep the names of the medication, the dates and times taken, and what effects you observe. You may also want to keep notes on the dates and results of other kinds of treatment, such as therapy and hospitalization. This kind of information is critical to share with the child's physician in deciding whether changes or adjustments are necessary. Having to recall dates and behaviors can be difficult, particularly considering all the other stresses that come with caring for a bipolar child. Documentation helps insure accuracy, and that can make a difference in how soon the child can move toward improvement and get on the road to a better quality of life.

# XI. Know Your Rights

The American system of government makes provisions for its citizens who have mental and physical disabilities. There are laws regarding employment, education, privacy, civil rights, and the rights of families. Like most legalities, these laws and regulations are complex. Parents are not required to be experts in the law, but public and some private agencies and institutions must not only understand these laws, they must practice them. For parents, just knowing that these laws exist and understanding some of the basic provisions can be a powerful tool when seeking services for children.

One of the most fundamental rights of children with mental disorders is the right to a quality education. Sadly, for decades many students with undiagnosed and untreated mental disorders have been labeled, isolated, and effectively robbed of the education that can help assure a higher quality of life.

Far from being "bad, sad, can't add," a phrase born of uninformed and frustrated professionals in the education system, studies have shown that given the right educational approaches, children with mental disorders can achieve.

*"Even as I write these words, my child, now approaching adulthood, forgets her medication, gets into physical confrontations, associates with people I don't approve of, and, because of unpredictable outbursts or failure to follow through on commitments, has difficulty holding a job.*

*Still, one thing I was always sure of was that she needed to graduate from high school with at least a 3.0 GPA. That may seem like a shallow, even inappropriate goal, given her condition, but I knew my child was bright, and I knew she could succeed in school.*

*Everything I knew told me to maintain high expectations, at least academically."* —*Cassandra Joubert*

Tremendous strides have been made and progress continues with stricter enforcement, updates and improvements of legal protections and provisions for eligible children, particularly in free, public education systems. Even private schools that receive federal funds are governed by regulations that require certain accommodations for eligible special education students.

In an interview, Ms. Joubert's most passionately expressed hope was that parents and educators would understand the absolute importance of a quality education for bipolar children. Learning and learning to think and imagine are important for any person's success and growth as a human being. Interestingly enough, as with special children, such as those who are bipolar, autistic, or labeled "idiot savant," there is often a modicum of genius. Some researchers have found that bipolar children are especially creative. What this means is that with treatment for the illness and a solid education, or at least an appreciation for lifelong learning, there is no limit to the variety of contributions a bipolar person could make to society.

Many public schools in urban and rural areas struggle under the disparity of resources and that can be frustrating for parents seeking quality services for their special needs children. Regardless of the level at which resources start, the goal must always be to acquire the best available for the child. If one school system has inadequate resources, look for open enrollment opportunities in alternative schools or systems in other communities.

Ms. Joubert believes that teachers also can make a difference. As they say, all it takes is one good teacher with a commitment to find the services for one special needs child. The results will multiply into services for even more children.

In 1975, the United States Congress enacted the Education for All Handicapped Children Act (Public Law 94-142) signed by President Gerald Ford. Amendments in 1990 changed the name to the Individuals with Disabilities Education Act (IDEA).

IDEA includes protections for children with mental disorders and emotional or behavioral problems. The act was reauthorized in 2004 by Congress and President George Bush.

Part B of IDEA mandates that a free, appropriate public education (FAPE) be provided to all children with disabilities from age three to age twenty-one. State laws vary on the upper age limit. The provisions are detailed and cover a range of services.

Past abuses, misinformation, and stigma have given "special education" a bad name, when in fact, if appropriately applied, "special education" can mean higher levels of achievement for children diagnosed with mental illnesses and disorders.

Special education is not designed to label children as "slow" or to isolate them from other students, but rather to provide the environment, curriculum, schedule, and activities that minimize the effects mental illnesses have on learning and behavior. As with any child, education is an important part of development, growth, and the ability to function in adulthood.

Parents can turn to their local school or state education system for full explanations and provisions of education laws. The first step is to obtain an assessment to determine whether your child is eligible for the "special education" services. If a child has been diagnosed with a mental illness or a parent suspects something is wrong, a request for an assessment can be made to the child's teacher, school principal, or the director of special education at the local or state level.

If the child is determined to be eligible, the local school district is required to hold a meeting within thirty days of the eligibility determination to formulate an individualized education program (IEP) for the child.

The IEP is a critical part of a child's overall treatment success and should be developed with much thought and consideration for the individual child's needs and interests where appropriate. The plan development team should include parent(s), teachers, and any other required representatives. If the parent and school staff disagree on the IEP's contents, the parent has a right to a due process hearing before an impartial hearing officer.

Part C of IDEA contains provisions for early intervention from birth to age two for infants and toddlers with disabilities. Evaluations and services are obtained through the state lead agency. The lead agency can be the State Department of Education, a health or human services department, or other agency. Parents unsure of a state's lead agency for infant and toddlers with disabilities can find the proper contact through their state's Office of the Governor.

If a child does not qualify for services under IDEA, there is a possibility that special services can be obtained under Section 504 of the Rehabilitation Act of 1973. Programs that receive federal funds through the U.S. Department of Education arc also required under Section 504 to provide a free appropriate public education (FAPE) to qualified students in the school district's jurisdiction.

The U.S. Department of Education monitors school district compliance with these important federal laws through its Office of Special Education Programs (OSEP). If a school district is not in compliance, a parent can contact the OSEP customer service specialist for their state.

In 2004, nearly 1.4 million African American children ages three to twenty-one received services under Part B of IDEA, according to the U.S. Department of Education, Office of Special Education Programs, Data Analysis System (DANS) 2004 report. Each parent who asserts the rights provided under IDEA and Section 504, helps move the nation a step closer to true equal education access for children with mental healthcare needs.

Individuals with Disabilities Education Act (IDEA) and Section 504 are actually provisions of the Americans with Disabilities Act (ADA), a group of wide reaching federal laws that protect the civil rights of individuals with disabilities.

"A Guide to Disability Rights Laws, September 2005," a publication of the U.S. Department of Justice, Civil Rights Division, Disability Rights Section, gives a very readable summary of the many provisions of ADA. The guide begins with this summary of the Act:

**Americans with Disabilities Act (ADA)**

*The ADA prohibits discrimination on the basis of disability in employment, State and local government, public accommodations, commercial facilities, transportation, and telecommunications. It also applies to the United States Congress.*

*To be protected by the ADA, one must have a disability or have a relationship or association with an individual with a disability. An individual with a disability is defined by the ADA as a person who has a physical or mental impairment that substantially limits one or more major life activities, a person who has a history or record of such an impairment, or a person who is perceived by others as having such an impairment. The ADA does not specifically name all of the impairments that are covered.*

*A free, complete copy of the guide and other materials regarding the Americans with Disabilities Act can be obtained from the U.S. Department of Justice by calling the ADA Information Line at 1-800-514-0301 or 1-800-514-0383 (TDD), or by visiting the Americans with Disabilities Act website at www.ada.gov.*

# XII.  Parent as Advocate

As parents find their way through the mental healthcare maze, some emerge with a conviction to not only seek change for the sake of their own loved ones, but for all children and families. Ms. Joubert chose to educate others through telling her story. Others find their own ways to make their voices for change heard. Any parent with the determination and the right tools and information can become an advocate for the care and protection of children with mental healthcare needs.

Webster's Dictionary defines an advocate as, "One that pleads the cause of another." Individuals from a variety of professional backgrounds are continuously working to bring about change in the nation's mental healthcare system. These advocates include educators, social workers, physicians, nurses, law enforcement staff, community leaders, and others. Parents are valuable members of these advocacy groups because they can most passionately express the human toll the system's inadequacies have on families and children like Maya.

Many parents have already found ways to become involved in these efforts, but many others hesitate out of fear they aren't educated enough or smart enough to be taken seriously. But anyone can gain the skills they need for advocacy.

The first step is to know the issues. Information from a variety of sources is available on all aspects of the mental healthcare debate. Parents can search the internet, visit the public library, or obtain information by contacting federal and state agencies. Many will mail free copies of reports, studies, fact sheets, and a variety of other resources. The child's physician should also be able to provide information. Advocate parents should learn how widespread the problems are, what effects the issues have on children, families, and society as a whole, the causes of the problems, and be able to offer some solutions. Once armed with knowledge, parent advocates can begin to take action.

There are so many ways parents can make their voices heard. An action as simple as writing a letter to local or state elected officials, from school board members all the way up to the governor, can begin to open the door to change. Be persistent. If no response comes the first time, write again or take it a step further and encourage family, friends, church members, and others to write letters also.

When writing a letter or email, keep it simple and civil. Be courteous. Politicians, as any human being would, prefer to respond to a reasonable request rather than a sheet of paper full of accusations and scorn. In the first paragraph, identify the reason for writing. In subsequent paragraphs, include information and examples of why the issue is of such importance. Offer resolutions to the problem. And before mailing or hitting the "send" button, proofread and spell-check the work. For those who include a full name, address, and telephone number, the likelihood of getting a response is increased.

Parents can form advocacy groups by engaging the participation of other families with similar needs, concerned friends, and community leaders, or they can join coalitions that already exist.

The media can also be useful in bringing about change. Parents can connect with the media by writing or calling local papers, and radio and TV stations to suggest or request coverage of the issue or cause. The media can raise awareness, spread knowledge, change public attitudes, and encourage action. Articles or news stories on the cause or project can also help identify other supporters. Sometimes those who read or watch the story will send financial support, letters of encouragement, or lead to other individuals who want to participate in the cause.

Finally, parent advocates should be prepared for the long haul. Real change generally does not come easily or quickly. The legislative processes of local and federal governments are themselves slow and arduous. Even when new laws are passed, full implementation can take years. But the citizens of this nation would not have the protections gained thus far if individuals and groups advocating for change had not remained committed to the cause.

It is critical to ask a lot of questions, network, talk to everyone, know the issues, keep track of progress, and remain optimistic.

# XIII. Improving Our Systems of Care and Support

---

*"If we don't stand up for children, then we don't stand for much."* —*Marian Wright Edelman*

---

Families cannot be left alone to shoulder the responsibility of fundamental change in the nation's mental healthcare systems. The Report of the Surgeon General's Conference on Children's Mental Health, a supplement to The Surgeon General's report of 1999 and the President's New Freedom Commission on Mental Health, 2002 both found major deficiencies at nearly every level of service.

These reports revealed that in many ways, mental healthcare providers, advocates, juvenile justice officials, and other stakeholders are as much victims of our entangled systems and institutions as children and families. In some instances, the frustrations and complications they face while trying to serve clients are overwhelming.

Most importantly, through the work of well-qualified and committed panels of experts, these reports also set improvement goals and made important recommendations for change, identifying steps that various agencies, institutions, and policy makers can take to improve care and simplify access to services. With all stakeholders working together, a redesigned system can be created.

The Report of the Surgeon General's Conference on Children's Mental Health set a National Action Agenda that identified eight major goals:

**1. Promote public awareness of children's mental health issues and reduce stigma associated with mental illness.**

The steps recommended for achieving this goal included the promotion of social, emotional, and behavioral well-being as an essential part of healthy development in children; the creation of child development enhancement guidelines, with separate, relevant guidelines tailored to each group—the public, families, caregivers, and professionals; the identification of early indicators of mental health problems; the inclusion of mental health assessment as part of a child's overall healthcare; the development of a "national capacity" to provide preventive mental healthcare; and the development of a public education campaign to counter the stigma attached to mental illness.

**2. Continue to develop, disseminate, and implement scientifically proven prevention and treatment services in the field of children's mental health.**

A list of action steps includes the support of numerous areas of research into the prevention and treatment of childhood mental disorders, with assessment of long-term and short-term outcomes; the development of model programs that can be used at the community level; and the development of partnerships, forums, and workgroups where information and findings can be shared between researchers, providers, and families.

**3. Improve the assessment and recognition of mental health needs in children.**

The report recommends, among other actions, that early identification be encouraged at several points of contact with children, including preschool, childcare, school systems, and health, welfare, and juvenile justice agencies. It also recommended that tools be created to help the professionals in these systems assess children, and primary healthcare providers and education staff be trained to recognize early indicators of mental disorder.

**4. Eliminate racial/ethnic and socioeconomic disparities in access to mental healthcare.**

The recommended actions include increasing the accessibility of culturally competent, scientifically proven services that take into account the strengths and needs of children and families; increased recruitment and training of providers from the racial, ethnic, and cultural groups that represent the nation's diversity. Other actions toward this goal call for the development of policies for uninsured children and more research that will help eliminate racial, ethnic, gender, sexual orientation, and socioeconomic disparities in diagnosis, prevention, and delivery of services.

**5. Improve the infrastructure for children's mental health services including support for scientifically proven interventions across professions.**

The report encourages universal, comprehensive, and continuous health coverage for mental health prevention and treatment. A review of the incentives and disincentives for healthcare providers to provide mental health assessment is recommended, as is the creation of incentives and resources for agencies, programs, and individuals to bring proven intervention strategies into local community settings.

## 6. Increase access to and coordination of quality mental healthcare services.

This goal is accompanied by a long list of recommendations starting with the development of a common way of describing children's mental issues and a universal age appropriate, culturally competent, and gender sensitive measurement system to identify children who need mental healthcare services and to track progress during treatment and individual treatment outcomes. It also suggests that services be provided in settings used regularly by children and families, including school, recreation centers, and churches, and to include them in discussions on setting the national mental healthcare agenda.

## 7. Train frontline providers to recognize and manage mental health issues, and educate mental health providers in scientifically proven prevention and treatment services.

Frontline providers across a variety of systems should receive training in child mental health enhancement and be provided with the skills to detect early symptoms so that intervention occurs earlier. The frontline providers include healthcare professionals, emergency room staff, educators, daycare staff, and juvenile justice personnel. The training should focus on, "developmental and cultural differences in cognitive, social, emotional, and behavioral functioning, and understanding these issues in familial and ecological context," the report states. In addition, the shortage of well-trained child mental health specialists, particularly among minorities, should be addressed.

**8. Monitor the access to and coordination of quality mental health-care services.**

Formal partnerships need to be formed between federal research, regulatory and service agencies, professional associations, and families/caregivers to share knowledge related to children's mental health, and service coordination and access equity efforts should be monitored, the report states. This section also recommends accountability strategies, provider-to-consumer education on the effectiveness or shortcomings of various treatments, and services and mechanisms for disseminating information on effective prevention and treatment through a variety of stakeholders.

The Surgeon General's conference report recommendations are in line with the findings and goals described in the "Outline of the Final Report for the President's New Freedom Commission on Mental Health," which begins with this vision statement:

*"We are committed to a future where recovery is the expected out-come and when mental illness can be prevented or cured. We envision a nation where everyone with a mental illness will have access to early detection and the effective treatment and supports essential to live, work, learn, and participate fully in their community."*

Both reports are insightful sources of information for all stake-holders interested in understanding the fundamental weaknesses of the nation's mental healthcare systems and for supporting efforts to redesign services. These reports are the results of months of discussion, research, and collaboration between well-qualified participants from a cross-section of professionals, advocates, and consumers. The recom-mendations should not be set aside to gather dust in some governmental archive. Rather, they should serve as architectural plans for building a better mental healthcare model for children or anyone trapped in a frightening cycle of untreated mental illness.

Copies of the full reports can be downloaded from the Web sites of the U.S. Surgeon General's Office and the Presidential Commission.

# XIV. Resources

Many resources provide useful information for families with children suffering from bipolar disorder and other mental illnesses. These resources offer consumer education on mental illnesses and treatments, connections to support groups and advocacy efforts, contacts for federal agencies that regulate and monitor mental health services and protections, and much more. This is a partial guide and most of the entries listed here provide links to additional resources. The Internet is full of information that can be obtained just by entering key search terms. Families without Internet access in the home can often access the Internet through computer services at public libraries. The following list of resources may also be helpful.

**24-Hour National Suicide Hotlines**
1-800-SUICIDE (1-800-784-2433)
1-800-273-TALK (1-800-272-8255)

**Depression and Bipolar Support Alliance**
1-800-826-3632
www.ndmda.org

**National Medical Association**

(Source for finding African American doctors)

1-888-662-7497

www.nmanet.org

**Black Psychiatrists of America**

(510) 834-7103

**Association of Black Psychologists**

P.O. Box 55999

Washington, D.C. 20040-5999

Phone: (202) 722-0808

www.abpsi.org

**American Association of Pastoral Counselors**

Phone:  (703) 385-6967

www.aapc.org

**American Psychiatric Association (APA)**

1000 Wilson Blvd.

Suite 1825

Arlington, VA 22209

**(APA) Answer Center**

Phone (USA) 1-888-35-PSYCH

Phone outside USA (703) 907-7300

www.healthyminds.org

**National Alliance for the Mentally Ill (NAMI)**
2107 Wilson Blvd., Suite 300
Arlington, VA 22201-3042
Phone Help Line: 1-800-950-NAMI (6264)
www.nami.org

**National Mental Health Association (NMHA)**
2000 N. Beauregard St., 6th Floor
Alexandria, Virginia 22311
Phone: 1-800-969-NMHA (6642)
www.nmha.org

## RESOURCES FROM OFFICE OF THE U.S. SURGEON GENERAL

**Center for Mental Health Services (CMHS)**
National Mental Health Information Center
P.O. Box 42557
Washington, DC 20015
Phone: 1-800-789-2647
www.mentalhealth.samhsa.gov

**National Institute of Mental Health (NIMH)**
Office of Communications and Public Liaison
6001 Executive Blvd.
Room 8184, MSC 9663
Bethesda, MD 20892-9663
Phone: (301) 443-4513
www.nimh.nih.gov

**Administration for Children and Families**
370 L'Enfant Promenade, S.W.
Washington, DC 20447
www.acf.dhhs.gov

**National Center on Minority Health and Health Disparities**
6707 Democracy Blvd., Suite 800
Bethesda, MD 200892-5465
Phone: (301) 402-1366
http://ncmhd.nih.gov

**Office of Minority Health Resource Center**
**U.S. Department of Health and Human Services**
P.O. Box 37337
Washington, DC 20013-7337
Phone: 1-800-444-6472
www.omhrc.gov

**Office of Minority Health**
Rockville, MD 20857
5600 Fishers Lane, Room 10-75
Phone: (301) 443-7265

**SAMHSA's National Mental Health Information Center**
www.mentalhealth.samhsa.gov

**The Society for the Psychological Study of Ethnic Minority Issues**
Division 45 of the American Psychological Association
www.apa.org/divisions/div45

Each state has one or more parent centers that provide a variety of services for families with children and youth from birth to age twenty-two who have disabilities. To locate a state's parent center contact:

**National Technical Assistance Center**
**PACER Center**
8161 Normandale Blvd.
Minneapolis, MN 55437-1044
Phone:  1-888-248-0822
Web Site: www.taalliance.org

# Works Cited

"A Guide to Disability Rights Laws, September 2005, U.S. Department of Justice, Civil Rights Division, Disability Rights Section

African American Community Mental Health Fact Sheet; National Alliance on Mental Illness, Multicultural Action Center.

Akiskal, HS Mood Disorders: Introduction and Overview, Comprehensive Textbook of Psychiatry, Kaplan and Sadock, 7th edition, 2000, p.1284-1298

*America's Children: Key National Indicators of Well Being,* Federal Interagency Forum on Child and Family Statistics, 2005

Annie E. Casey Foundation, Key Indicators of Child Well-Being, 2003-2004

Baldassano CF. Illness course, comorbidity, gender, and suicidality in patients with bipolar disorder J Clin Psychiatry. 2006;67 Suppl 11:8-11

Baldassano CF, Marangell LB, Gyulai L, Nassir Ghaemi S, Joffe H, Kim DR, Sagduyu K, Truman CJ, Wisniewski SR, Sachs GS, Cohen LS. Gender differences in bipolar disorder: retrospective data from the first 500 STEP-BD participants. Bipolar Disord. 2005 Oct;7 95): 465-70

Birmaher B, Axelson D, Strober M, Gill MK, Valeri S, Chiappetta L, Ryan N, Leonard H, Hunt J, Iyengar S, Keller M Clinical course of children and adolescents with bipolar spectrum disorders. Archives of General Psychiatry, Feb 2006 63(2):175-183

Blumber HP, Kaufman J, Martin A, Whiteman R, Hongyuan JZ, Gore JC, Charney DS, Krystal JH, Peterson BS Amygdala and Hippocampal Volumes in Adolescents and Adults with bipolar disorder Arch Gen Psychiatry. 2003;60:1201-1208

Cartwright, S "Diseases and Peculiarities of the Negro Race", DeBow's Review-Southern and Western Stories, Vol.XI, New Orleans, 1851

Chang KD, Steiner H, Ketter TA Psychiatric phenomenology of child and adolescent offspring J Am Acad Child Adolesc Psychiatry, 2000 April 39 (4):453-460

Chang, KD,Blasey, Steiner H, and Ketter TA. Temperament characteristics of child and adolescent bipolar offspring, 2003 J Affect Disord 77:11-19

Child and Adolescent Bipolar Disorder: An Update from the National Institute of Mental Health Fact Sheet, 2000

Coyle JT, Pine D, Charney DS, Lewis L, Nemeroff CB, Carlson GA, Joshi PT, Reiss D, Todd RD, Hellander M: Depression and Bipolar Support Alliance Consensus Development Panel J Am Acad Child Adolesc Psychiatry.2003;42 (12):1494-1503

Delbello MP, Strakowski SM. Understanding the problem of co-occurring mood and substance use disorders. In: J Westermeyer& R Weiss, eds. Integrated Treatment for Mood and Substance Use Disorders, Johns Hopkins Press, 2002

DelBello MP, Hanseman D, Adler CM, Fleck DE, Strakowski SM. Twelve-month outcome of adolescents with bipolar disorder following first hospitalization for a manic or mixed episode. Am J Psychiatry.2007 Apr; 164 (4): 582-90

Diagnostic and Statistical Manual for Mental Disorders, fourth Edition American Psychiatric Association, Washington, DC

Epidemiologic Catchment Area Study, 1980-1985, study no. 6153

Frazier JA, Ahn MS, DeJong S, Bent EK, Breeze JL, Giuliano AJ. Harv Rev Psychiatry. 2005 May-June;13 (3) 125-40

Freeman MP, Smith KW , Freeman SA, McElroy SL, Kmetz GE, Wright R, Keck PE. The Impact of Reproductive Events on the Course of Bipolar Disorder in Women. J. Clin Psychiatry, 2002 Apr:63 (4): 284-7.

Garno JL, Goldberg JF, Ramierez PM, Ritzler BA Impact of childhood abuse on the clinical course of bipolar disorder. et al, Br J Psychiatry 2005 Feb:186:121-5

Geller B, Luby J, Child And Adolescent Bipolar Disorder: A Review of the Past 10 Years. J Am Acad Child Adoles Psychiatry 36:1997, pp.1168-1176

Geller B, Zimmerman, et al. "Diagnostic Characteristics of 93 Cases of a Prepubertal and Early Adolescent Bipolar Disorder Phenotype by Gender, Puberty, and Comorbid Attention Deficit Hyperactivity Disorder." Journal of child and Adolescent Psychopharmacology 10 (2000): 157-164

Geller B, Zimmerman, et al. "DSM-IV Mania Symptoms in a Prepubertal and Early Adolescent Bipolar Disorder Phenotype Compared to Attention-deficit Hyperactive and Normal Controls."Journal of Child and Adolescent Psychopharmacology 12 (2002)

Gershon ES, Hamovit JH, Guroff JJ, Nurnberger JI Birth-cohort changes in manic and depressive disorders in relatives of bipolar and schizoaffective patients. 1987 Arch Gen Psychiatry 44:314-319

Goldstein TR, Birmaher B, Axelson D, Ryan ND, Strober MA, Gill MK, Valeri S, Chiappetta L, Leonard H, Hunt J, Bridge JA, Brent DA, Keller M. History of suicide attempts in pediatric bipolar disorder: factors associated with increased risk, Bipolar Disord. 2005 Dec:7 (6):525-35

Goldstein TR, Axelson DA, Birmaher B, Brent D. Dialectical Behavior Therapy for Adolescents with bipolar disorder: a 1 year open trial. 2007 J. Am Aca. Child Adolesc. Psychiatry, 46:7, July, 820-830

Hirschfeld RM, Calabrese JR, Weissman MM, Reed M,Davies MA, Frye MA, Keck PE, Lewis L, McElroy SL, McNulty JP, Wagner KD. Screening for bipolar disorder in the community. J Clin Psychiatry. 2003 Jan:64 (1):53-9

*Incarceration of Youth Who Are Waiting for Community Mental Health Services in the United States;* Special Report, United States House of Representatives Committee on Government Reform – Minority Staff Special Investigations Division, July 2004, prepared for Rep. Henry A. Waxman and Sen. Susan Collins.

Individuals with Disabilities Education Act (IDEA) 1990

Jackson V, "In Our Own Voices: African American Stories of Oprression, Survival, and Recovery in the Mental Health System, p. 1-36

Jones BE, Gray, BA, Problems in Diagnosing Schizophrenia and Affective Disorder Among Blacks, Hosp Community. Psychiatry 1986 Jan; 37(1):61-5

Kessler RC, Chiu WT, Demler O, Walters EE. Prevalence, Severity, and Comorbidity of 12-month DSM-IV disorders in the National Comorbidity Survey Replication (NCS-R). Archives of General Psychiatry, 2005 Jun; 62 (6):617-27

Key Issues, National Center for Mental Health and Juvenile Justice: Key Issue 2

Kowatch R Conditions and Diagnoses: Bipolar Disorder, Cincinnati Children's Hospital Medical Center Fact Sheet, July 31, 2006

Kowatch R, Youngstrom E, Danielyan A, and Findling R. Review and meta-analysis of the phenomenology and clinical characteristics of mania in children and adolescents. Bipolar Disorder 2005 Dec:7(6):484-96

Kupfer DJ, Frank E, Grochocinski VJ, Houck PR, Brown C. African-American participants in a bipolar disorder registry: clinical and treatment characteristics. Bipolar Disord. 2005 Feb;7 (1):82-8

Lange KJ, McInnis MG. Studies of anticipation in bipolar affective disorder. CNS spectrum 2002 Mar;7(3):196-202

Lapalme M, Hodgins S, LaRoche C. Children of parents with bipolar disorder: a metaanalysis of risk for mental disorders. Can J Psychiatry.1997 Aug:42 (6): 623-31

Leibenluft E, Rich B, Vinton D, Nelson E, Fromm, S, Berghorse L, Joshi P, Robb A, Schachar R, Dickstein D, McClure E, Pine D; Neural Circuitry Engaged during unsuccessful motor inhibition in pediatric bipolar disorder Am J Psychiatry 2007;164:52-60

Leibenluft E, Charney DS, Pine D. Researching the pathophysiology ofpediatric bipolar disorder. 2003 So Biol Psychiatry 53:1009-1020

Leverich GS, McElroy Sl, Suppes T, Keck PE Jr, Denicoff KD, Nolen WA, Altshuler LL, Rush AJ, Kupka R, Freye MA, Aution KA, Post RM, Early physical and sexual abuse associated with an adverse course of bipolar illness. Biol Psychiatry 2002 Feb 15;51(4):288-97

Leverich GS, Post RM , Keck PE Jr., Altshuler LL, Frye MA, Kupka RW, Nolen WA,, Suppes T, McElroy SL, Grunze H, Denicoff K, Moravec MK, Luckenbaugh D, The poor prognosis of childhood-onset bipolar disorder J Pediatr 2007 May:150(5) 485-90.

Lawson. DEPRESSION AND MOOD; Culture, Biology, and Treatment-Implications for African Americans. Presented at the National Medical Association, Region IV Meeting, Aug. 2006

Luby JL,et al. Preschool bipolar disorder: assessment and validation. Presented at the Annual Meeting of the American Academy of Child and Adolescent Psychiatry, Oct.21, 2005

Luby JL, Heffelfinger AK, Mrakotsky C, Brown KM, Hessler MJ, Wallis JM, Spitznagel EL. The clinical picture of depression in preschool children. Journal of the American Academy of child and Adolescent Psychiatry, vol.42:3, pp.340-348, March 1, 2003

Manji JK, Grand Rounds, University of California, Los Angeles Neuropsychiatric Institute, 2003

McQueen, MB, Devlin B. Faraone SV et al. Combined analysis from eleven linkage studies of bipolar disorder provides strong evidence of susceptibility loci on chromosomes 6q and 8q. American Journal of Human Genetics 2005 Oct: 77(4):582-95.

Mental Health America. 10-year Retrospective Study Shows Progress in American Attitudes About Depression and Other Mental Health Issues, June 6, 2007

National Institutes of Mental Health Fact Sheet, 2006

National Institute of Mental Health Research Roundtable on Prepubertal Bipolar Disorder. (2001) American Academy of Child and Adolescent Psychiatry, 40,871-878

Paplos, D, Paplos J. The Bipolar Child. New York: Broadway Books, 1999

Paplos D, Hennen J, Cockerham MS, Thode HC Jr., Youngstrom EA. The child bipolar questionnaire: a dimensional approach to screening for pediatric bipolar disorder. J Affect Disorder. 2006 Oct;95(1-3):149-58. Epub 2006 June 23

Pavuluri MN, Birmaher B, Naylor M: Pediatric bipolar disorder: Ten year review. J Am Acad Child Adolesc Psychiatry 2005:44:846-871

Perlis RH, Miyahara S, Marangell Lb, Wisniewski SR, Ostacher M, DelBello MP, Bowden CL, Sachs GS, Nierenberg AA:Step BD Investigators. Long-Term implications of early onset in bipolar disorder: Data from the first 1000 participants in the systematic treatment enhancement program for bipolar disorder (STEP-BD) 2004 Biol Psychiatry;55(9):875-881

Practice Parameters in Diagnosis and Treatment of Bipolar Disorder in Children and Adolescents. 2007 Am Acad Child and Adol Psych January 46 (1) 107-125

President's New Commission on Mental Health, October 29, 2002.

President's New Freedom Commission on Mental Health, October 2002, Page 4, *A Fragmented Mental Health System*

Regier DA, Farmer ME, Rae DS, Locke BZ, Keith SJ, Judd LL, Goodwin FK. Comorbidity of mental disorders with alcohol and other drug abuse. Results from the Epidemiologic Catchment Area (ECA) Study. JAMA 1990; 264:pp 2511-2518

Rich BA, Vinton DT, Roberson-NayR, Hommer RE, Berghorst LH, McClure EB, Fromm SJ, Pine DS, Leibenluft E. Limbic hyperactivation during processing of neutral facial expressions in children with bipolar disorder. Proceedings of the National Academy of Sciences USA 2006 June 6:103(23):8900-5 Epub 2006 May 30

Scrambler PJ, Kelly D, Lindsay E, Wiliamson R, Goldberg R, Shprintzen R, Wilson DI, Goodship JA, Cross IE, Burn J, Lancet 1992,339: May 9 1138-1139

Strakowski SM, Keck PE, etc. Ethnicity and First-rank Symptoms in Patients with Psychosis, J Clin Psychiatry, 2003 Jul; 64(7):747-54

Strakowski, McElroy, Keck PE, West SA, Racial Influence on Diagnosis in Psychotic Mania. J. Affect Disorder. 1996 Jul 8;39(2):15

Strober M, Schmidt-Lackner S, Freeman R, Bower S, Lampert C, DeAntonio M,. Recovery and relapse in adolescents with bipolar affective illness: a five-year naturalistic, prospective follow-up. J Am Acad Child Adolesc Psychiatry 34:724-731 Wash U. BPD in Preschoolers

U.S. Department of Education, Office of Special Education Programs, Data Analysis System (DANS) 2004

U.S. Public Health Service, Report of the Surgeon General Conference on Children's Mental Health: A National Agenda. Washington, DC: Department of Health and Human Services, 2000.

Wozniak J, Spencer T, Biederman J, et al. The clinical characteristics of unipolar vs. bipolar major depression in ADHD youth. J Affect Disord. 2004;821 suppl:559-569

# About the Authors

 **Dr. Cassandra Joubert** is the parent of two won-
derful children, Josh and Maya. She is married
and resides with her husband and daughter in
Beverly Hills, Michigan. Dr. Joubert received her
undergraduate degree in psychology and child
development from Howard University in Washington, DC. She received the Doctor of Science
degree in maternal and child health from the Johns Hopkins School of
Hygiene and Public Health. She has worked in the fields of children's
health, community planning, minority health, child advocacy, and aca-
demia, and most recently, in philanthropy.

**Dr. Linda Thompson Adams, DrPH, RN,** is Professor and Dean of
the School of Nursing at Oakland University in Auburn Hills, Michigan. She is a graduate of the School of Hygiene and Public Health at
Johns Hopkins University, and Wayne State University School of Nursing. Dr. Thompson Adams has been the principal investigator on several community-based research and demonstration programs funded
by public and private sources to improve the health of women and
children. Through her work, Dr. Thompson Adams has examined critical public health issues such as problem behaviors in adolescents, the
use of neighborhood health advocates in the delivery of services, and
control of intentional injuries among adolescent males. Her research

on the health needs of incarcerated children resulted in publication of a book entitled *Hard Time, Healing Hands: Developing Primary Health Care Services for Incarcerated Youth*. This book received an honorable mention in the Distinguished Service Award category from Washington Ed Press for outstanding treatment of a major public concern.

**Dr. Janice Hutchinson** is Assistant Professor of Psychiatry and Pediatrics at Howard University, Washington, DC. She is also Secretary and DC Legislative Representative from the Washington Psychiatric Society. Dr. Hutchinson is the Residency Training Director in Psychiatry. She is board certified in Pediatrics, Adult and Child Psychiatry.

Special interests upon which she has lectured and written include child abuse, domestic violence, teen pregnancy, HIV/AIDS, antidepressant use in children, impulsivity and aggression in children, incarcerated youth and mental illness and suicide among youth. Research projects have included Systemic Treatment Enhancement Program for Bipolar Disorder (STEP-BD), Collaborative Genomic Study of Bipolar Disorder, and Adolescents at High Risk for Familial Bipolar Disorder. In 2005 she was among AMA's Irma Bland Excellence in Teaching Award recipients. International medical practice has also been part of her experience, having worked in Liberia and in Thailand. Dr. Hutchinson is a Chicago native who attended Stanford University as an undergraduate and University of Cincinnati Medical School. She trained in Pediatrics both at Montefiore/Einstein and at Rush Presbyterian. She also trained in Adult Psychiatry at both University of Cincinnati and St. Elizabeth's Hospital. She completed a Child and Adolescent Fellowship at Institute for Juvenile Research. Dr. Hutchinson earned a Masters in Public Health at the University of Illinois.

Printed in the United States
103040LV00002B/58-165/A